The People's Bible Teachings

JUSTIFICATION

How God Forgives

Wayne D. Mueller

NORTHWESTERN PUBLISHING HOUSE
Milwaukee, Wisconsin

Scripture taken from the HOLY BIBLE, NEW INTERNATIONAL VERSION®. Copyright © 1973, 1978, 1984 by International Bible Society. Used by permission of Zondervan Publishing House. All rights reserved.

The "NIV" and "New International Version" trademarks are registered in the United States Patent and Trademark Office by International Bible Society. Use of either trademark requires the permission of International Bible Society.

All rights reserved. No part of this publication may be reproduced, stored in a retrieval system, or transmitted in any form or by any means—electronic, mechanical, photocopying, recording, or otherwise—except for brief quotations in reviews, without prior permission from the publisher.

Library of Congress Control Number: 2001135253
Northwestern Publishing House
1250 N. 113th St., Milwaukee, WI 53226-3284
© 2002 by Northwestern Publishing House
http://www.nph.net
Published 2002
Printed in the United States of America
ISBN 0-8100-1369-X

Table of Contents

Editor's Preface 5

Introduction 7

1. What Do We Mean by Justification? 10
2. Why Do We Need to Be Justified by God? 22
3. What Moves God to Justify Us? 34
4. Whom Does God Justify? 48
5. Who Benefits from Justification? 56
6. How Long Does It Take to Be Justified? 68
7. What Also Happens When We Are Justified? 76
8. What Do Our Good Works Have to Do with Justification? 92
9. What Is the Current Status of the Justified? 100
10. What Is the Final Status of the Justified? 116

    Endnotes 125

    For Further Reading 127

    Scripture Index 129

    Subject Index 135

Editor's Preface

The People's Bible Teachings is a series of books on all of the main doctrinal teachings of the Bible.

Following the pattern set by The People's Bible series, these books are written especially for laypeople. Theological terms, when used, are explained in everyday language so that people can understand them. The authors show how Christian doctrine is drawn directly from clear passages of Scripture and then how those doctrines apply to people's faith and life. Most importantly, these books show how every teaching of Scripture points to Christ, our only Savior.

The authors of The People's Bible Teachings are parish pastors and professors who have had years of experience teaching the Bible. They are men of scholarship and practical insight.

We take this opportunity to express our gratitude to Professor Leroy Dobberstein of Wisconsin Lutheran Seminary, Mequon, Wisconsin, and Professor Thomas Nass of Martin Luther College, New Ulm, Minnesota, for serving as consultants for this series. Their insights and assistance have been invaluable.

We pray that the Lord will use these volumes to help his people grow in their faith, knowledge, and understanding of his saving teachings, which he has revealed to us in the Bible. To God alone be the glory.

Curtis A. Jahn
Series Editor

Introduction

"If the doctrine of justification is lost, the whole of Christian doctrine is lost."[1] This is how Martin Luther expressed the central importance of the Bible's teaching of justification. The faithful men who later committed Luther's Bible teachings to formal confessions made a similar assertion. They taught that the church stands or falls on the teaching of justification.

Justification is the Bible's technical word for how God forgives. The Bible uses many different word pictures to assure us of God's forgiveness. Remission, redemption, reconciliation, atonement, cleansing (washing, purging), taking away, and forgetting are some of the most common ones. But the word *justification* literally explains how it was possible for a just and holy God to embrace condemned sinners to himself in Jesus Christ.

Justification is a legal word that embodies the whole heart and action of God in reconciling sinners to himself. It resolves the Scripture's tension between law and gospel, between the holiness and the grace of God. In doing so, justification draws the Bible's entire message into a divinely coherent unity.

Justification is the core of the gospel's message. That we might be justified by faith is the reason God sent Jesus. Justification is the gospel blossom the Holy Spirit brought to full bloom in Saint Paul's New Testament letters. For 14 centuries after that, however, the fragrance of God's message was increasingly masked with human error. By the Middle Ages, justification's meaning and thus its comfort were barely discernable to clergy or laity. Then, through his servant, Martin Luther, God once again uncovered his precious flower. The Lutheran Reformation unfolded justification in shining new clarity for the church.

Satan knows that the message of how God forgives the sinner is the heart of the gospel. So he attacks justification with greater vehemence than he does any other teaching, save that of the person of Jesus Christ himself. Since the Reformation, Satan has pushed forward Arminianism, dead orthodoxy, Pietism, rationalism, liberalism, Fundamentalism, sectarianism, humanism, modernism, and Eastern mysticism in his attempt to push the church back into the spiritual darkness of the Middle Ages.

In post-Christian America, many congregations are struggling to maintain or regain their vitality. Clergy libraries are full of books about how churches can pull themselves up by their bootstraps. But the real answer to the inner and outer vigor of the church lies here, in the clear proclamation of justification by grace alone, by Christ alone, through faith alone. The church's high calling in every age is to defend and disseminate the teaching of justification against every effort of Satan. That is how God reinvigorated the church through Paul and through Luther. This is the message by which God will restore vitality to his church today.

We remember, however, that God's church is the gathering of many individual believers into Christ's body. For each of us individual believers, justification holds the highest importance. When God justified you and me, God reestablished the relationship between himself and us sinners. So justification by Christ alone is the centerpiece of personal faith. From justification every blessing of God flows to you and me. Paul wrote: "Therefore, since we have been justified through faith, we have peace with God through our Lord Jesus Christ, through whom we have gained access by faith into this grace in which we now stand. And we rejoice in the hope of the glory of God" (Romans 5:1,2).

Thus this book. As long as justification is preached by Christ's church and trusted by the individual believer, Satan is stymied. And he knows it. This book aims to help the individual believer and the gathered church in their struggle against the onslaughts of the gates of hell. This book intends neither to embellish nor to expand on justification but merely to let it shine in the simple splendor the Holy Spirit has already given it. It is written with the prayer that God will renew our faith in his declaration of righteousness for us and will give us courage to continue to proclaim justification to the world.

What do we mean by justification?

It is God's declaration of forgiveness.

1

What Do We Mean by Justification?

The meaning of the word

Justification is just one of many terms the Bible uses to tell us that God has forgiven our sins. Although it is found elsewhere, it is used mostly by Paul in his letters to the Romans and Galatians. The word *justification* is special because it not only announces God's forgiveness, it also explains in a technical way how God forgives us. Justification encompasses the meaning of the various scriptural words and phrases for forgiveness. It draws into itself God's whole plan of salvation as fulfilled by Jesus Christ.

For this reason, in the Lutheran church, the word *justification* is synonymous with forgiveness. From a positive point of view, justification is pregnant with comforting assurance of God's grace to the sinner. It is the heart and core of the gospel. From a negative standpoint, justification argues against all the wrong ideas about salvation and forgiveness that Satan has raised against it, inside and outside of the visible church.

To justify means literally to declare righteous. Scripture teaches that in his mercy God declares the sinner to be righteous for Christ's sake, through faith. By grace alone, God pronounces us holy, innocent, and morally perfect. From this truth is derived the hallmark teaching of the Lutheran Reformation: justification by Christ alone, by grace alone, by faith alone. "We . . . know that a man is not justified by observing the law, but by faith in Jesus Christ" (Galatians 2:15,16).

Justification is a forensic term. This means that Paul borrowed it from the language used in public debate and law courts. When a court justifies a defendant, it declares him to be "not guilty," innocent of the crime or crimes with which he is charged. In Paul's day, just as in legal proceedings today, this justification was a verdict or pronouncement of the court.

Understanding the forensic nature of justification is key to understanding its meaning in the Bible. A court's pronouncement is legal, not medicinal. That means that the court's decree of innocence changes neither the past actions nor the present moral quality of the defendant. A pronouncement of "not guilty" does not alter the accused person's actual guilt or innocence. The only thing that forensic justification changes is the status of the accused in the eyes of the court. The innocent verdict declares how the court will act toward the defendant. When the accused is judged to be innocent, he is treated from that point on as such, regardless of past or present conduct. He is set free. He is not punished for his crimes. And he cannot be held accountable for them again at a future time.

This understanding of justification has become a part of the official teachings of the Lutheran church. The Lutheran Confessions say, "We believe, teach, and confess that according to the usage of Scripture the word 'justify' means in this article 'absolve,' that is, pronounce free from sin."[2]

Justification is the heart of the gospel

Justification is the word the Bible uses to tell us what God has done for us in Christ. For the sake of Jesus' perfect life and sacrificial death, God has declared us innocent of all the sins we commit. This means that regardless of past actions or present moral character, we are now free of the guilt of our sin. We are released from any punishment for our sin. This declaration by God is the gospel, the good news of our forgiveness.

Believers of all time were and are saved only by this pronouncement of God that they are innocent for Christ's sake. To the Jews at Rome, Paul argued that the patriarchs Abraham and David were saved by the same gospel that he was now preaching to them in the name of Christ. Quoting from Genesis chapter 15, Paul wrote: "What does the Scripture say? 'Abraham believed God, and it was credited to him as righteousness'" (Romans 4:3). Referring to Psalm 32, Paul pointed out that King David was saved by the same proclamation: "David says the same thing when he speaks of the blessedness of the man to whom God credits righteousness apart from works" (Romans 4:6).

An Easter proclamation

When did God pronounce this "not guilty" verdict? On Easter morning God declared all the world justified by the life, death, and resurrection of Jesus Christ. Jesus' resurrection was God's final proof to the world that God had accepted the life and death of his Son for our salvation.

When he preached in Pisidian Antioch, Paul tied the resurrection of Jesus to our justification: "But the one whom God raised from the dead did not see decay. Therefore, my brothers, I want you to know that through Jesus the forgiveness of sins is proclaimed to you. Through him everyone who believes is justified from everything you could not be justified from by the law of Moses" (Acts 13:37-39). Again, in his letter to Corinth, Paul said that our forgiveness hinges on Jesus' resurrection: "If Christ has not been raised, your faith is futile; you are still in your sins" (1 Corinthians 15:17). Finally, in his letter to the Roman Christians, Paul once more connected Christ's resurrection to our justification: "The words 'it was credited to him' were written not for him alone, but also for us, to whom God will credit righteousness—for us who believe in him who raised Jesus our Lord from the dead. He was delivered over to death for our sins and was raised to life for our justification" (Romans 4:23-25).

Of course, forgiveness through Jesus Christ was an accomplished fact in the heart of God from eternity. This is why Paul could write that God for Christ's sake justified Old Testament believers like Abraham and David before Jesus appeared in history. Yet we may think of Easter morning as the time in history when God made his formal declaration of righteousness for sinners.

An alien righteousness

Lutherans refer to the righteousness God declared for sinners as an alien righteousness. That means that the righteousness that we now possess by faith through justification is a righteousness that has a source outside of ourselves. Nothing that we are or do contributes to it. The decree of innocence that God issues for Christ's sake is not contingent on anything good that is inherent in us or anything good that we have merited through our actions.

The concept that the righteousness we receive from God in justification comes from outside of us and not from within us was the heart of Luther's faith in salvation. In his commentary on Galatians, he wrote, "By the one solid rock which we call the doctrine of justification we mean that we are redeemed from sin, death, and the devil and are made partakers of life eternal, not by ourselves . . . but by help from without, by the only-begotten Son of God, Jesus Christ."[3]

Human beings did at one time have an inherent righteousness. At the beginning, when God created us, he made us in his own holy image. We were personally righteous, without sin. But Adam and Eve lost their personal righteousness when they fell into sin. So Holy Scripture makes it clear that the righteousness God now credits to us in justification is alien to us. It is not inherent in us. It is not our own personally earned righteousness. When Paul spoke to the Philippians about his personal faith, he said he wanted to "gain Christ and be found in him, not having a righteousness of [his] own that comes from the law, but that which is through faith in Christ—the righteousness that comes from God and is by faith" (Philippians 3:8,9).

So the righteous decree God made on Easter morning had nothing to do with something good in us or something good we had done in obedience to the law. This is a constant theme in Paul's epistles. To the Romans he wrote, "But now a righteousness from God, apart from law, has been made known, to which the Law and the Prophets testify. This righteousness from God comes through faith in Jesus Christ to all who believe" (Romans 3:21,22). Even the thought that we may earn or supplement God's righteousness puts us at risk of losing his grace: "You who are trying to be justified by law have been alienated from Christ; you have fallen away from grace" (Galatians 5:4).

The Bible's message regarding this alien righteousness that God credits to us produced a great awakening in Martin Luther. Recall that for years Luther struggled with a false concept of righteousness. Raised in the Roman Catholic tradition, he connected the Bible's every mention of justice and righteousness to God's demand for his personal obedience to the law. Try as he would, he could not find peace of conscience in his rigorous attempts to keep God's commandments. Bible passages such as, "The righteous will live by . . . faith" (Habakkuk 2:4; Romans 1:17), frightened him. He reasoned that if he was not personally just, or righteous, he was not living by faith.

Through his study of the Bible, especially the books of Romans and Galatians, Luther came to a right understanding of the gospel. God led him to understand that saving righteousness was not from himself; it was "a righteousness from God" (Romans 1:17; 3:21). "In the Scriptures," Luther wrote, "the righteousness of God is almost always taken in the sense of faith and grace, very rarely in the sense of the sternness with which He condemns the wicked and lets the righteous go free."[4] "But he is discussing righteousness in the sight of God, by which we are freed from the Law, sin, death, and every evil, become partakers of grace, righteousness, and life, and eventually are established as the lords of heaven and earth and of all creatures. This righteousness neither human nor divine Law is able to produce."[5]

So Luther could join with Paul's confession: "I do not set aside the grace of God, for if righteousness could be gained through the law, Christ died for nothing!" (Galatians 2:21). When commenting on this passage, Luther wrote, "This means that you will not be a Christian unless you cast away your own righteousness entirely and rely on faith alone."[6]

How Scripture uses the word

The Bible uses *justification* in the simple sense of being declared righteous. Justification means the same as being forgiven. Jesus said in regard to the humble tax collector who prayed for forgiveness in the temple: "I tell you that this man, rather than the other, went home justified" (Luke 18:14). Paul used the word with this plain meaning in Romans 5:1: "Therefore, since we have been justified through faith, we have peace with God through our Lord Jesus Christ."

Justification also means forgiveness when the Bible says that God credits righteousness through faith. Paul used this phrase several times in Romans chapter 4. First he quoted Genesis 15:6 in regard to Abraham: "Abraham believed God, and it was credited to him as righteousness" (verse 3). Then he applied the principle to all who believe: "To the man who does not work but trusts God who justifies the wicked, his faith is credited as righteousness" (verse 5). Going back to Abraham's faith, he wrote:

"This is why 'it was credited to him as righteousness.' The words 'it was credited to him' were written not for him alone, but also for us, to whom God will credit righteousness" (4:22-24). This crediting is accounting terminology. On our personal record, where our sin had created a huge deficit, God credits the righteousness of Jesus. What we did not earn is credited to our account as though we ourselves had earned it.

The change that justification brings

One more thing about justification needs to be stressed. We have said that God's justifying the sinner is like a judicial decree that does not change the actual moral fiber of the defendant. On the other hand, we must note that justification does not produce a change in God either. God does not change. God still hates and punishes sin. God still desires our personal righteousness.

So, if justification does not change us or God, then what does change when we are justified? Justification changes our status before God's court of justice. It changes our relationship to him. When God declares us not guilty, he sets us free. He promises never to punish us. When he says he will not remember our sins (Jeremiah 31:34), he is promising that he will not return later and charge us with that which he has forgiven.

Commenting on 2 Corinthians 5:18, Professor John Meyer wrote:

> There are some who assume that [reconciliation] points to a change in God, that during the process He changed from an irate into a placated God, that some sort of appeasement took place.—But no, not the least change took place in the heart of God. It was His love which was active dur-

ing the entire process of [reconciliation]. The change was effected in our status before our Judge.⁷

Reconciliation is one of the words the Bible uses to indicate our change in status before God. Paul wrote: "Since we have now been justified by his blood, how much more shall we be saved from God's wrath through him! For if, when we were God's enemies, we were reconciled to him through the death of his Son, how much more, having been reconciled, shall we be saved through his life!" (Romans 5:9,10). God "reconciled us to himself through Christ and gave us the ministry of reconciliation: that God was reconciling the world to himself in Christ, not counting men's sins against them" (2 Corinthians 5:18,19).

When sinful people are reconciled with a holy God, a radical change in status has taken place. "Once you were alienated from God and were enemies in your minds because of your evil behavior. But now he has reconciled you by Christ's physical body through death to present you holy in his sight, without blemish and free from accusation" (Colossians 1:21,22).

Thus justification is not a medicine God prescribes to fix something inside us. His decree does not change our inner moral character or improve our disposition toward him. Instead, justification restores a relationship that our sinful actions and our natural evil disposition had ruined.

The cornerstone of the church's teaching

Until the end of time, the teaching of justification will remain the cornerstone doctrine of Christ's church. Luther insisted, "The doctrine of justification must, as I frequently urge, be diligently learned; for in it all the other articles of our faith are comprehended. And when that is safe, the others are safe too."[8] We can trace the modern decline of the visible Christian church to the way it waters down or outrightly denies justification by Christ. Luther would have agreed:

> In short, if this article concerning Christ—the doctrine that we are justified and saved through Him alone and consider all apart from Him damned—is not professed, all resistance and restraint are at an end. Then there is, in fact, neither measure nor limit to any heresy and error.[9]

What God led Luther to treasure in his heart became the great treasure of the Lutheran church through the reformer's teachings and writings. The Lutheran Confessions say, "This article of justification by faith is 'the chief article of the entire Christian doctrine,' 'without which no poor conscience can have any abiding comfort or rightly understand the riches of the grace of Christ.'"[10]

Those who bemoan the sad state of affairs in much of the visible church today must take notice. When faith flourishes in the hearts of individual believers, the outward church will again see God's blessing.

Why do we need to be justified by God?

Sin keeps us from justifying ourselves.

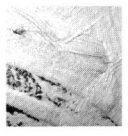

2

Why Do We Need to Be Justified by God?

Worldly justification

We live in a world of justification—not God's kind, but man's kind. Immersed in godless immorality, people's consciences drive them to look for ways to justify or defend their aberrant behavior. Sadly, pagans look everywhere but to God to be assured that they are innocent.

Although there are many variations, there are four basic ways that our sinful nature seeks to be justified: rationalizing, denying, blaming others, and comparing. There is nothing new about any of these human means of self-justification. Every beginner course on human psychology should require a careful study of Genesis chapter 3.

There Adam and Eve evidence all four approaches to self-justification after their fall into sin.

Rationalizing

During Satan's temptation, Eve justified her sin by rationalizing. "The fruit of the tree was good for food," she reasoned with herself, "pleasing to the eye, and also desirable for gaining wisdom" (Genesis 3:6). We may safely imagine that Eden contained hundreds, if not thousands, of beautiful trees. And they all bore perfect fruit. God had not forbidden eating from any of them except the tree of the knowledge of good and evil. Yet note Satan's fiendish audacity. He approached Eve with the unreasonable suggestion that God was holding back some pleasure or being unfairly restrictive by his demands. "He [Satan] said to the woman, 'Did God really say, "You must not eat from any tree in the garden"?'" (Genesis 3:1).

All sin is at its root illogical. Eve fell into sin when the unreasonable became reasonable to her and she ate of the tree. But what Eve did not realize until it was too late is that what seemed sensible to her was merely sinful rationalization. She sinned against the First Commandment when she doubted the clear word of her God.

The modern day maxim "If it's fun, it must be sinful" shows that we have inherited Eve's propensity for rationalization. We foolishly imagine that we know better than God what is good for us. "God made his laws to keep us from enjoying ourselves," our sinful nature argues. But our failure to trust God's good intentions toward us is just as much a sin against the First Commandment now as it was in the garden. Solomon wrote, "There is a way that seems right to a man, but in the end it leads to death" (Proverbs 14:12).

Situational ethics is a prominent example of the rationalization of sin. Even when ugly consequences prove situational choices wrong, its self-justifying alibi paraphrases Eve's: "It seemed like the right thing to do at the time." The basis of situational ethics is the assumption that human beings possess the rational ability to make the best choice for themselves in any circumstance. But this assumption flies in the face of God's assessment of human reason. Paul wrote, "The sinful mind is hostile to God. It does not submit to God's law, nor can it do so. Those controlled by the sinful nature cannot please God" (Romans 8:7,8).

Because our judgment is clouded by sin, we cannot trust our good sense to determine what is right and wrong. Our sinful nature makes it impossible to justify our actions with logic. When we offer one empty self-justification after another, we demonstrate that we do not even know that our rationalizations are irrational to a holy God. Just as Eve experienced and Solomon warned, our sinful rationalizations lead to death.

Denying

Another way we seek to justify ourselves is denial. Adam and Eve sewed fig leaves together to cover themselves. Then they tried to hide from God among the trees of the garden. They tried to make believe it never happened. Think of how far they had fallen! From the perfect knowledge they possessed in God's image at creation, they devolved to absurdly thinking that they could hide from God. One moment they elevated their human reason above God's command, and the next instant they denied the commonsense reality of their transgression. This is classic denial. It's making believe that we didn't sin or that we can escape the consequences of our sin.

Trying to justify sinful actions with unreasonable denial is a common human course since the fall. Adam and Eve passed on to us not only their sinful guilt and liability for punishment. They also bequeathed to us their natural proclivity to sin. That is why you and I are still inclined to stubborn denial. We hate to admit that we are wrong about anything. We are quick to condemn, but slow to confess.

But stonewalling God and denying our sin does not make it go away. Foolishly, we may each try to hide from God behind the trees of our gardens. But God sees. "Nothing in all creation is hidden from God's sight. Everything is uncovered and laid bare before the eyes of him to whom we must give account" (Hebrews 4:13). Saint John warns, "If we claim to be without sin, we deceive ourselves and the truth is not in us. If we claim we have not sinned, we make him out to be a liar and his word has no place in our lives" (1 John 1:8,10).

It's bad enough when our own sinful nature leads us individually to deny our transgressions. It is even worse when churches publicly aid and abet that denial with false teaching. Among many supposedly Christian denominations today, gross sins such as fornication, homosexuality, unscriptural divorce, and even abortion are openly condoned, even endorsed. No one will seek true justification in the life and death of Jesus if they become hardened in self-justification through denial. As Armin Schuetze has written, "The full scope of man's sin and God's righteous wrath against sin must be recognized as a presupposition to an understanding of the doctrine of justification and an appreciation for it."[11]

More insidious than tolerating actual sins, but just as destructive, is the denial of original sin by many traditional mainline churches. Denial of original sin is a trademark of many otherwise conservative, evangelical Bible Belt denominations. This false teaching contradicts clear biblical testimony: "Like the rest, we were by nature objects of wrath" (Ephesians 2:3). Denying original sin gives rise to the false premise that after the fall we still have the ability to make a decision for Christ. It also prevents our confession of sins from being wholly honest. Similarly the Roman Catholic Church sustains the notion that sinners can play a part in their own justification.

For this reason, in our Lutheran churches, we make a double confession of sins every week. In varying wording, our liturgies lead us to confess, "I confess that I am by nature sinful and that I have disobeyed you in my thoughts, words, and actions."[12] This full confession—of both our sinful nature and sinful action—opposes worldly self-justification. It admits that we have not done anything and do not have the natural ability to do anything that will justify our past sins. Through this confession, the Spirit prepares us to rest our hearts and our hopes entirely on the justification that God alone can provide in Christ alone.

Blaming others

Blaming others is the third way the godless mind of man seeks to justify itself. It is childish finger pointing. Notice Adam's reply when God confronted him about his sin in the garden: "The woman you put here with me—she gave me some fruit from the tree" (Genesis 3:12). Adam is actually pointing two fingers of guilt, one at Eve and another at God.

Notice the demonic deviousness in the progression of self-justification on the part of Adam and Eve. "It seemed like the right thing at the time. . . . We didn't really do it. . . . Well, if we did do it, it was somebody else's fault." We see this progression of thought at work in our society too. Situational ethics is rationalization. Denial goes a step further when it gives approval to gross sins like homosexuality and abortion. But shifting the blame takes us still further downhill when we blame our parents, the government, and society for the mess our sins have gotten us into.

This is the sad story of sinful mankind's approach to justification since the fall. But we must go beyond accepting this as a general principle. We must take it to heart personally. We believers have a sinful nature that depletes our strength to fight the good fight of faith and hold on to God's justification. This means that we who have been justified by Christ still at times sinfully seek to justify ourselves.

Finger pointing diminishes our sanctified efforts at living for Christ. Cliques within congregations try to assign blame for problems to other factions or individuals. We disrupt our Christian homes when husbands and wives, children and parents project their guilt on one another. Daily we must confess our efforts to shift the blame, and by faith we must grasp again the only justification that avails before God, justification by Christ alone.

Comparing

There is one more kind of human self-justification. That is justification by comparing ourselves with others. This was the means by which the Pharisee sought to justify himself before God: "God, I thank you that I am not like other men—robbers, evildoers, adulterers—or even like this tax collector. I fast twice a week and give a tenth of all I get" (Luke 18:11,12). Adam's shifting of the blame for his guilt onto his wife and God was also a form of justification by comparison. He reasoned that even if he was guilty of sin, God, who put his wife with him in the garden, and his wife, who tempted him, should bear greater burdens of guilt.

Unfortunately, this age-old dodge is still alive and kicking today. The man who excuses his absence from worship by condemning all the hypocrites in the congregation is justifying himself by comparison. So is the worshiper who feels smug about her own life when she hears the pastor condemn the gross sins of the outside world. So am I, and so are you, when we, in any way, feel secure that God accepts us because we are better than others.

The 18th-century hymn "Rock of Ages, Cleft for Me" is placed in the category of "Justification" hymns in *Christian Worship: A Lutheran Hymnal* ([CW] 389). Stanza 3 presents the attitude of faith that serves as the antidote for us who lapse into justification by comparison:

> Nothing in my hand I bring,
> Simply to thy cross I cling;
> Naked, come to thee for dress,
> Helpless, look to thee for grace.
> Foul, I to the fountain fly—
> Wash me, Savior, or I die!

Whenever we seek to justify ourselves by comparison, we reveal our ignorance about God and his law. The sinful reasoning that God should look favorably on us because we are better than others completely misses the point. The point is that God's law demands not comparative goodness but absolute perfection. Jesus said, "Be perfect, therefore, as your heavenly Father is perfect" (Matthew 5:48). The holy God requires more than that we be nice. When evaluating ourselves, God demands that we compare ourselves to him and not to other sinful humans.

A story is told of Dr. Dwight Moody, founder of the Moody Bible Institute in Chicago. As he and a student were walking home one evening after classes, they encountered a drunk lying in a gutter, facedown in his own vomit. The student, seeking to elicit a favorable comment on his own level of sanctification, said, "How disgusting! I cannot even imagine how a man can fall to such depths." Dr. Moody, however, responded more humbly. "There," he said, "but for the grace of God go I."

In his epistle Saint James was dealing with strife and favoritism among Christian worshipers. James did not want them to make the mistake of trying to justify themselves by comparing themselves with others. He wanted them to understand that greed and selfish ambition were no more commendable than theft and robbery. Gossip, finger pointing, and cursing are as damnable as lying and slander. Adultery is as bad as murder. Fighting and arguing is pagan conduct. When we compare ourselves favorably to others, we mistakenly rank sins in order of importance. But James wrote, "For whoever keeps the whole law and yet stumbles at just one point is guilty of breaking all of it" (James 2:10). Paul agreed: "All who rely on observing the law are under a curse, for it is written: 'Cursed is everyone who does not continue to do everything written in the Book of the Law.' Clearly no one is justified before God by the law, because, 'The righteous will live by faith'" (Galatians 3:10,11).

Not worldly but heavenly justification

None of Adam and Eve's attempts at self-justification availed. God rejected their rationalizing, their denying, their blaming others, and their comparing themselves to others. But Adam and Eve were justified. They were justified through their faith in God's promised Savior.

Before he wrote his great discourse on justification in Romans chapters 3 to 5, Paul prepared the hearts of his readers by ridding them of any hope of justifying themselves. In chapter 1 he argued that the pagan Romans, because of their idolatry and gross sins, had no hope of standing approved before God. Then in chapter 2 he made it clear that the Jews, steeped in Old Testament law, had no better hope of justifying themselves. For the Jews, even though they knew the law of God inside and out, were unable to keep it.

What was Paul's conclusion? "Therefore no one will be declared righteous in his sight by observing the law; rather, through the law we become conscious of sin" (Romans 3:20). The law is not there to justify us in the sight of other people. It is there to show us that we cannot justify ourselves in "his sight"—that is, God's sight.

The Holy Spirit has also led us to this same conclusion. Before he could lead us to faith in "a righteousness from God, apart from law," he had to convince us that "no one will be declared righteous by observing the law." "An understanding of this [man's sin and the holiness of God] is a necessary presupposition for a correct understanding of the justification of man before God."[13]

Luther's approach to preparing the heart for justifying faith imitated Paul's:

> Now the true meaning of Christianity is this: that a man first acknowledge, through the Law, that he is a sinner, for

whom it is impossible to perform any good work. For the Law says: 'You are an evil tree. Therefore everything you think, speak, or do is opposed to God. Hence you cannot deserve grace by your works.' . . . When a man is taught this way by the Law, he is frightened and humbled. Then he really sees the greatness of his sin and finds in himself not one spark of the love of God; thus he justifies God in His Word and confesses that he deserves death and eternal damnation. Thus the first step in Christianity is the preaching of repentance and the knowledge of oneself.[14]

Think of how God has brought us to faith in Christ. He began by convincing us that we could not justify ourselves before God. From that we learn how we may in turn become God's instruments to share justification by Christ with others. Before the Holy Spirit brings other people to faith, he will, through our witness, convince them that all the man-made attempts at justification leave a person without appeal before God's judgment seat. Then the Holy Spirit will convince the hearts of others, as he once led ours, to accept the only righteousness that counts in God's court.

What moves God to justify us?

God justifies us for Christ's sake.

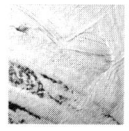

3

What Moves God to Justify Us?

God's mercy and justice

Our God is loving and holy. "The LORD is righteous in all his ways and loving toward all he has made" (Psalm 145:17). Love and perfection are not mere attributes or characteristics of God. His grace and his holy justice are his very essence. "God is love" (1 John 4:16). "Holy, holy, holy is the LORD Almighty" (Isaiah 6:3; Revelation 4:8).

We humans can sometimes act out of character. We are able to do things that contradict our general attributes. But God cannot do anything contrary to what he is. "For he cannot disown himself" (2 Timothy 2:13). Because we are human and sinful, God's love and moral perfection can appear to be two different things. Sometimes God's mercy and justice seem to contradict each other. Adam and Eve, for instance, fell into sin when God's holy command about the tree seemed to contradict his love for them.

But in God there is no such contradiction. Everything God is and does demonstrates perfect love and absolute holiness. "For the LORD is righteous, he loves justice" (Psalm 11:7). This truth finds its highest expression in the way God dealt with the problem of our sin. By sending his Son, Jesus Christ, to be our Savior, God demonstrated to the world that any conflict between his perfect love and his perfect justice is only apparent.

God's plan of salvation

God's love moved him to plan our salvation. "For God so loved the world," Jesus explained to Nicodemus, "that he gave his one and only Son" (John 3:16). When God looked ahead from eternity and saw that his highest creatures would fall into sin, his heart of love prompted him to devise a plan of salvation for the human race. We know his divine plan was in place before he created mankind, because he tells us that he elected believers to salvation in Jesus before the beginning of the world. "He [God] chose us in him [Christ] before the creation of the world to be holy and blameless in his sight. In love he predestined us to be adopted as his sons through Jesus Christ, in accordance with his pleasure and will" (Ephesians 1:4,5).

But to understand justification, we must remember that God's love always acts in accord with his holiness. His gracious plan to save us could not contradict his righteous demand that his human creatures be morally perfect. "I am the Lord your God," he tells his people. "Consecrate yourselves and be holy, because I am holy" (Leviticus 11:44). His merciful plan to forgive sinners could not diminish the punishment his holy justice required of us.

People with a shallow understanding of forgiveness imagine that God displays his love without justice. They portray God as a kindly old grandfather who cannot help overlooking the sins of his little ones. They erroneously define forgiveness as the triumph of God's love over his holiness. This false piety believes that if we can emotionally wrench ourselves into abject sorrow for our wrongdoings, God's heart will melt and he will have to forgive us.

But we cannot appease God's holy justice with tearful appeals to his love. This kind of thinking denies God's righteous justice. It is just another subtlety Satan uses to make us believe we have a role in gaining God's favor. It divides God against himself and against what he reveals about his essential nature in the Bible.

Our groveling—no matter how intense—can never resolve the tension the sinner feels between God's mercy and justice. Our sorrow for sin does not precipitate God's forgiveness. God's plan of salvation revealed in sacred Scriptures insists that only Jesus Christ can do that. God's desire to forgive sinners began in eternity and was carried out through Jesus Christ. "He was chosen before the creation of the world" (1 Peter 1:20). "He made known to us the mystery of his will according to his good pleasure, which he purposed in Christ" (Ephesians 1:9). "While we were still sinners, Christ died for us" (Romans 5:8). God sent Jesus because only Jesus could demonstrate God's love with justice. "He did it to demonstrate his justice at the present time, so as to be just and the one who justifies those who have faith in Jesus" (Romans 3:26).

Jesus fulfilled God's plan

In order to justify the sinner, God sent a Savior who embodied both his love and his holiness. In love he sent a Savior who was himself God, because no person is able to save him- or herself, much less others or the whole human race. "No man can redeem the life of another or give to God a ransom for him—the ransom for a life is costly, no payment is ever enough—that he should live on forever and not see decay" (Psalm 49:7-9). Jesus came as true God to demonstrate a divine love that no human was able to do. "From the fullness of his grace we have all received one blessing after another. For the law was given through Moses; grace and truth came through Jesus Christ. No one has ever seen God, but God the One and Only, who is at the Father's side, has made him known" (John 1:16-18). God's love sent a Savior who is divine.

On the other hand, God's holiness demanded that the Savior be fully human. God's righteous law required perfect human obedience and human death as punishment for disobedience. "Cursed is everyone who does not continue to do everything written in the Book of the Law. Christ redeemed us from the curse of the law by becoming a curse for us, for it is written: 'Cursed is everyone who is hung on a tree'" (Galatians 3:10,13). In order to fulfill God's holy demand for human perfection, Jesus became fully human to take our place under the law. God's holiness sent a Savior who is human.

God wants us to trust that his justification of sinners is both loving and holy. He wants us to believe that such justification came about only through Jesus Christ, the God-man. This is why Scripture repeatedly proclaims Jesus to be fully divine and fully human. Isaiah predicted the Savior's coming: "For to us a child is born, to us a son is given.

... And he will be called Wonderful Counselor, Mighty God, Everlasting Father" (Isaiah 9:6). John began his gospel with a clear statement: "The Word was God. The Word became flesh and made his dwelling among us" (John 1:1,14). Matthew gave the same testimony at the birth of Jesus: "'They will call him Immanuel'—which means, 'God with us'" (Matthew 1:23). In the upper room, Jesus stood before his disciple Philip in obvious human form and said to him, "Anyone who has seen me has seen the Father" (John 14:9). Paul asserted, "There is one God and one mediator between God and men, the man Christ Jesus" (1 Timothy 2:5).

Jesus obeyed to suffer our punishment

As true God and true man, Jesus came and carried out God's loving, holy plan to justify sinners. The Bible calls Jesus' saving work obedience. "When Christ came into the world, he said, . . . 'I have come to do your will, O God'" (Hebrews 10:5-7). Paul seemed to be talking about all of Christ's work when he wrote, "For just as through the disobedience of the one man the many were made sinners, so also through the obedience of the one man the many will be made righteous" (Romans 5:19).

Although the Bible does not use the exact words, Christian teachers refer to our Lord's compliance with the Father's will as his active and passive obedience. Jesus' passive obedience includes all those things he endured to take on himself the punishment of our sins. In his ministry he dealt with the consequences of sin: disease, death, and the injustice of others. He allowed suffering and death to come on himself. Isaiah predicted Jesus' quiet, passive obedience under suffering: "He was oppressed and afflicted, yet he did not open his mouth; he was led like a

[handwritten: Jesus submissiveness = his passive obedience]

lamb to the slaughter, and as a sheep before her shearers is silent, so he did not open his mouth. By oppression and judgment he was taken away" (Isaiah 53:7,8). In Gethsemane Jesus prayed in submission to his Father's saving will for mankind: "Father, if you are willing, take this cup from me; yet not my will, but yours be done" (Luke 22:42). "He humbled himself and became obedient to death—even death on a cross!" (Philippians 2:8).

With his passive obedience, Christ accepted the full force of God's perfect justice. Jesus took on himself all of God's righteous anger against the unrighteousness of mankind. Jesus became fully human so he could suffer this human death. "Since the children have flesh and blood, he too shared in their humanity so that by his death he might destroy him who holds the power of death—that is, the devil—and free those who all their lives were held in slavery by their fear of death" (Hebrews 2:14,15).

Repeatedly Scripture attests to the substitutionary nature of Christ's passive obedience. Jesus suffered all these things for us. "He was delivered over to death for our sins" (Romans 4:25). "God made him who had no sin to be sin for us" (2 Corinthians 5:21). "Christ died for the ungodly" (Romans 5:6). There, on the cross, Jesus suffered the very anguish of hell when he cried out, "My God, my God, why have you forsaken me?" (Matthew 27:46). "Christ redeemed us from the curse of the law by becoming a curse for us, for it is written: 'Cursed is everyone who is hung on a tree'" (Galatians 3:13).

Jesus passively submitted himself to all sufferings according to his true human nature. Yet Scripture assures us that Jesus participated in these sufferings also according to his divine nature, as God himself, in a way we cannot understand or explain. Paul wrote: "Be shepherds of the church of God, which he bought with his own blood" (Acts 20:28). Peter said to the Jews, "You killed the author of life" (Acts 3:15).

Our justification before God is based, in part, on Jesus' passive obedience. God declares us not guilty because the punishment for our sins has been paid for. Paul wrote, "Since we have now been justified by his blood, how much more shall we be saved from God's wrath through him!" (Romans 5:9). The Savior's obedience to God's plan of salvation has secured forgiveness. "Then he said, 'Here I am, I have come to do your will.'. . . And by that will, we have been made holy through the sacrifice of the body of Jesus Christ once for all" (Hebrews 10:9,10).

The blood of Jesus' passive obedience on the cross provided a cleansing from sin or a removal of sin. John the Baptist announced Jesus to the world in those terms: "Look, the Lamb of God, who takes away the sin of the world!" (John 1:29). In his great penitential psalm, King David expressed his trust in God's ability to remove his sins: "Cleanse me with hyssop, and I will be clean; wash me, and I will be whiter than snow" (Psalm 51:7). Paul wrote that Jesus gave himself up "to purify for himself a people that are his very own" (Titus 2:14). He said that in baptism Jesus cleansed his church "by the washing with water through the word" (Ephesians 5:26). John promised, "The blood of Jesus, his Son, purifies us from all sin" (1 John 1:7). In describing what Jesus did with our sins, the writer to the Hebrews said, "Christ was sacrificed once to take away the sins of many people" (Hebrews 9:28).

Jesus obeyed to give us righteousness

But the removal of our sin is only one aspect of the forgiveness we receive through justification. The term *justifi-*

cation introduces us to a deeper understanding of God's love for the sinner and a fuller appreciation of Jesus' saving obedience. The Bible uses the word *justification* to tell us that God's forgiveness is not only a subtraction of our sins. When God justifies us, he does something more than remove our sins. At the same moment he forgives us, he credits righteousness to us. A forgiven sinner is not merely an erased slate, a blotted out record. God also records into his account of our lives the perfection he had demanded of us under the law.

We said before that the righteousness God credits us in justification is an alien righteousness. That means the righteousness we possess through justification is not a moral perfection we produced in our own lives. Yet God accredits a holy life to us as though we ourselves had lived it. What is the source of this alien righteousness? To understand that, we have to look into what else the Scripture says about the obedience of Jesus Christ.

The same Jesus who passively obeyed his Father's saving will in suffering also actively obeyed his Father's saving will with perfect obedience to his law. The fully human Jesus actively obeyed his heavenly Father by living the righteous life the Father had demanded of us. Early in his ministry, Jesus indicated that this was the purpose for his life on earth. "Do not think that I have come to abolish the Law or the Prophets; I have not come to abolish them but to fulfill them" (Matthew 5:17).

Jesus became true man not only to take our place on the cross. He also came to be our substitute under the demands of God's law. His perfect life of obedience to God's commandments was an equal part of his redeeming work for us. That Jesus should live a holy human life was

What Moves God to Justify Us? 43

part of God's eternal plan and purpose for sending the Savior. "When the time had fully come, God sent his Son, born of a woman, born under law, to redeem those under law, that we might receive the full rights of sons" (Galatians 4:4,5).

Jesus' perfect obedience to God's law began publicly when he was circumcised on the eighth day as the Law of Moses demanded. "The parents brought in the child Jesus to do for him what the custom of the Law required" (Luke 2:27). At age 12, his appearance at the temple in Jerusalem, his desire to be about his Father's business, his obedience to his earthly parents, and his adolescent favor with God and man were all in accordance with the law (Luke 2:41-52). His baptism by John the Baptist was performed, in Jesus' own words, "to fulfill all righteousness" (Matthew 3:15).

Although Jesus was and is at all times both God and man, he humbled himself when he lived under the law as our perfect substitute. Beginning with his conception, he did not make full and continual use of his divine power as the God-man. The writer to the Hebrews tells us that Jesus' temptations to sin were just as intense as ours are: "We have one [Jesus the Son of God] who has been tempted in every way, just as we are—yet was without sin" (Hebrews 4:15). Jesus defeated Satan in the wilderness, not with his divine powers, but with the same power God put into the hands of every human to fight sin—simple little Bible passages. Jesus conducted his whole ministry without sin so that he was able to challenge his enemies, "Can any of you prove me guilty of sin?" (John 8:46). Jesus was not only the passive Lamb of God when he went to the cross. He was "a lamb without blemish or defect" (1 Peter 1:19), who had earned perfection.

Justification credits Jesus' righteousness to us

When the Bible says that God justifies us, it means that God credits this active obedience of Christ to the sinner. "Abraham believed God, and it was credited to him as righteousness. The words 'it was credited to him' were written not for him alone, but also for us, to whom God will credit righteousness—for us who believe in him who raised Jesus our Lord from the dead" (Romans 4:3,23,24). Just as the human death Jesus died substitutes for the death God demanded for our sins, so the holy life he led substitutes for the righteous life God demanded of us. "God made him who had no sin to be sin for us, so that in him we might become the righteousness of God" (2 Corinthians 5:21).

When God justifies the sinner, then, he does not only remove the guilt and punishment of our sin. At the same time that he forgives us, he credits to us the obedience Christ gave to the law as our substitute. As our Savior, Jesus satisfied God's holy demand for moral perfection.

The importance of Christ's active obedience

This Bible truth has been preserved by God in a special way in the Lutheran church. What Scripture says about Jesus' active obedience as our substitute under the law is often denied or ignored by Catholic and other Protestant churches. But for Lutherans, the fullness and clarity of justification shines through the perfect human obedience of our Savior. It helps us view the whole ministry and teaching of Jesus with new appreciation. We see everything Jesus did from conception to the cross as God's unified display of mercy with holiness. The guilty heart is drawn to the Jesus of the gospels with new hope. Every word Jesus speaks, every miracle, every act of kindness leads us to say, "He did this for me."

The Lutheran Confessions say about Jesus:

> His obedience consists not only in his suffering and dying, but also in his spontaneous subjection to the law in our stead and his keeping of the law in so perfect a fashion that, reckoning it to us as righteousness, God forgives us our sins, accounts us holy and righteous, and saves us forever on account of this entire obedience which, by doing and suffering, in life and in death, Christ rendered for us to his heavenly Father.[15]

Justification by Christ alone

We live in an age of pluralism in which all belief systems are deemed to have equal merit. In North America we see inroads cut into Christianity by Islam, Eastern mysticism, and Native American traditions. It is politically incorrect to assert the obvious, that is, that these conflicting religions cannot all be equally valid. Yet that is exactly what Scripture does when it asserts that justification is by Christ alone.

Nicodemus heard the simple alternatives from Jesus' own lips: "Whoever believes in him is not condemned, but whoever does not believe stands condemned already because he has not believed in the name of God's one and only Son" (John 3:18). The apostles likewise preached an exclusive message: "Salvation is found in no one else, for there is no other name under heaven given to men by which we must be saved" (Acts 4:12).

Paul, who had once pursued an alternative route to salvation, tied the exclusive nature of Christianity to the righteousness won by Christ. In his bold but humble confession of faith to the Philippians he wrote:

 Whatever was to my profit I now consider loss for the sake of Christ. What is more, I consider everything a loss

> compared to the surpassing greatness of knowing Christ Jesus my Lord, for whose sake I have lost all things. I consider them rubbish, that I may gain Christ and be found in him, not having a righteousness of my own that comes from the law, but that which is through faith in Christ—the righteousness that comes from God and is by faith. (Philippians 3:7-9)

Justification is by Christ alone because only Jesus exhibited the mercy and justice of God. God does not forgive, as all false religions imply, merely on the basis of his love. Luther had to deal with that kind of thinking already in his day. He wrote:

> There are some, especially among the modern, ranking schoolmen, who say: The forgiveness of sins and justification depend wholly and entirely on the divine imputation of grace, that is, on God's simply accounting as just, in spite of our sins. . . . Were this view true, the entire New Testament would really be vain and futile, and Christ would have labored foolishly and uselessly in suffering for sin. God Himself would have practiced jugglery and humbug without any need, because He might well have forgiven and not imputed sins without the suffering of Christ. Then some other faith, too, besides faith in Christ, might justify and save a man; I mean a faith that would simply rely on the gracious mercy of God, which would not hold his sins against him. . . . Now although out of pure grace God does not impute our sins to us, He nonetheless did not want to do this until complete and ample satisfaction of His Law and His righteousness had been made.[16]

Thus the only righteousness that avails before God on the last day is the righteousness of Christ credited to us in justification. The Lutheran hymn writer Paul Speratus set forth the active and passive obedience of Christ as his hope for the eternal future in two short stanzas:

Yet as the law must be fulfilled
Or we must die despairing,
Christ came and has God's anger stilled,
Our human nature sharing.
He has for us the law obeyed
And thus the Father's vengeance stayed
Which over us impended.

Since Christ has full atonement made
And brought to us salvation,
Each Christian therefore may be glad
And build on this foundation.
Your grace alone, dear Lord, I plead;
Your death is now my life indeed,
For you have paid my ransom. (CW 390:4,5)

Whom does God justify?

In Christ, God declares all to be righteous.

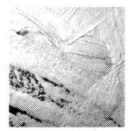

4

Whom Does God Justify?

God's universal love

Although salvation comes alone by Christ, the love of God who sent Jesus was not and is not exclusive. Jesus himself said so: "God so loved the world" (John 3:16). God's desire to save people is not limited to those who eventually believe. Paul instructs Timothy that God our Savior "wants all men to be saved and to come to a knowledge of the truth" (1 Timothy 2:4). Peter states God's universal love negatively and positively: "He is patient with you, not wanting anyone to perish, but everyone to come to repentance" (2 Peter 3:9).

God's heart has never desired that anyone should lose his or her salvation. God assured his Old Testament people: "For I take no pleasure in the death of anyone, declares the Sovereign LORD. Repent and live!" (Ezekiel 18:32). All these assurances of God's universal love for sinners would be empty if Christ's justifying work was not, in fact, declared for all people.

When Jesus came to earth, he came to be the Savior of all people of all time. John the Baptist pointed to him and said, "Look, the Lamb of God, who takes away the sin of the world!" (John 1:29). When Jesus died, "he died for all" (2 Corinthians 5:15). "Now he [Christ] has appeared once for all at the end of the ages to do away with sin by the sacrifice of himself" (Hebrews 9:26). "He is the atoning sacrifice for our sins, and not only for ours but also for the sins of the whole world" (1 John 2:2).

Lutheran teachers often call God's declaration of righteousness for all people *objective justification*. This means that God's Easter declaration of righteousness is an accomplished fact for all people, apart from the thinking or faith of people. Justification is a historical reality or an *object*, that is, independent of people. The ministry of the gospel of Jesus Christ is, essentially, the proclamation of objective justification to the world. Paul wrote that God "gave us the ministry of reconciliation: that God was reconciling the world to himself in Christ, not counting men's sins against them" (2 Corinthians 5:18,19). The message of the gospel is, in fact, this, that in Christ God justified the world.

Some false teachers have denied that God loves all. Still today, a branch of the Reformed church teaches that God predestined some people to hell. Some false teachers say that God loves all, but that Jesus' atonement was limited; he did not die for all. They believe he died only for those who eventually come to faith in him.

Lutherans generally agree that God loves all and that Jesus paid for the sins of all. But even among Lutherans there is not unanimous agreement that God declared all to be justified. The Lutheran Confessions, however, everywhere testify to objective justification. In the Formula of Concord, Article XI we confess: "Through Christ the human race has truly been redeemed and reconciled with God and . . . by his innocent obedience, suffering, and death Christ has earned for us 'the righteousness which avails before God' and eternal life."[17] We also read, "Hence if we want to consider our eternal election to salvation profitably, we must by all means cling rigidly and firmly to the fact that as the proclamation of repentance extends over all men (Luke 24:47), so also does the promise of the Gospel."[18]

In the Apology to the Augsburg Confession, Article IV, we make a similar confession:

> The law would seem to be harmful since it has made all men sinners, but when the Lord Jesus came he forgave all men the sin that none could escape and by shedding his blood canceled the bond that stood against us (Col. 2:14). This is what Paul says, "Law came in, to increase the trespass; but where sin increased, grace abounded all the more" (Rom. 5:20) through Jesus. For after the whole world was subjected, he took away the sin of the whole world, as John testified when he said (John 1:29), "Behold the Lamb of God, who takes away the sin of the world!"[19]

At the time of their ordination and/or installation, our Lutheran pastors and teachers willingly pledge themselves to these confessions of faith, secure in the knowledge that they present the truth of Scripture.

God's universal declaration

God's justification of the entire world is the simple, clear teaching of the Bible. Just as God loved all and Jesus died for all, God also declared all to be justified in the life and death of Christ. Right after writing that Jesus "died for all," Paul said, "God was reconciling the world to himself in Christ" (2 Corinthians 5:15,19). "For God was pleased to have all his fullness dwell in him, and through him to reconcile to himself all things, whether things on earth or things in heaven, by making peace through his blood, shed on the cross" (Colossians 1:19,20). When speaking of the results of Christ's obedience, the apostle said, "Consequently, just as the result of one trespass was condemnation for all men, so also the result of one act of righteousness was justification that brings life for all men" (Romans 5:18).

Those who deny that God declared all the world justified in Christ have a corrupted gospel to share with the world. If my forgiveness is not a fact unless and until I believe it, the gospel is conditional and thus not a simple proclamation of good news. My forgiveness then depends on something I do: my sorrow, my repentance, my faith. I make forgiveness happen by my believing. God's mercy to me depends on something other than Christ's obedience.

This is not the gospel Luther found in his Bible. When he penned the Large Catechism, he wrote in his explanation to the Fifth Petition: "Not that he [God] does not forgive sin even without and before our prayer; and he gave us the gospel, in which there is nothing but forgiveness, before we prayed or even thought of it. But the point here is for us to recognize and accept this forgiveness."[20]

Lutherans who try to separate Christ's universal sacrifice from God's objective declaration of forgiveness refer to the Lutheran Reformation's motto: "Justification by grace alone, by Christ alone, through faith alone." If justification is through faith alone, they argue, then no justification exists apart from faith.

But justification through faith alone was used by the reformers in a specific biblical and historical context. It was the rallying call of Lutherans of that time against all work-righteous approaches to salvation that the Bible condemns, and particularly against the mixing of works and faith in Roman Catholic theology. "Through faith alone" aimed to uphold Scripture's insistence that human works have no part in our forgiveness: "We maintain that a man is justified by faith apart from observing the law" (Romans 3:28). "Through faith alone" was coined to exclude all activity on the part of humans. Not a word from the mouth or pen of the reformers hints that "faith alone" ever was meant to exclude God's own declaration of forgiveness apart from faith.

By proclaiming *sola fide*, by faith alone, the reformers included other biblical truths about justification. For example, "through faith alone" does not set aside justification by grace alone or justification by Christ alone. In fact, salvation by grace alone rests on God's universal love for all people. Salvation by Christ alone stands on his universal payment for all the sins of all people. In the same way, salvation through faith alone rests on the truth that God's justification of the world is already an accomplished fact. Justification does not occur because of faith. To the contrary, faith grasps the justification that already exists.

Romans 5:12-19

Those who deny that God has justified all in Christ make much of Paul's use of the word *many* in Romans chapter 5, verses 15 and 19. In verse 19, Paul wrote, "For just as through the disobedience of the one man the many were made sinners, so also through the obedience of the one man the many will be made righteous." "See," they say, "Paul says that *many* will be made righteous through Christ, not *all*."

A closer look, however, shows that interpretation to be false. To know what Paul meant by *many* in this verse, we have to understand the use of the Greek word. The Greek word for many emphasizes "the large number referred to." It does not necessarily distinguish the many from most or all, as the word usually does in English. So, literally, the translation of the verse reads: "Through the obedience of the one man [Christ] a large number will be made righteous."

For that reason, only the context itself can determine whether the large number is all people or some of the people. In this verse, does *many* mean the large number of all human beings, or does it mean the large number of believers who trust that they have been justified?

Throughout this section (Romans 5:12-19), Paul compares Adam and Christ. Sin and death came through Adam; righteousness and life came through Christ. It is clear that God counted the sin of Adam against the whole human race. "Death came to all men, because all sinned" (verse 12). It is just as clear that God credits the righteousness of Christ to the whole human race in justification. "The result of one act of righteousness was justification that brings life for all men" (verse 18).

For the Roman congregation, made up of ethnic Jews and Gentiles, Paul wanted to stress the uniformity of God's universal justice. The Jews were willing to accept the Bible truth that God imputed the sin and punishment of one man, Adam, to the whole human race. But some of these same Jews were reluctant to accept that God included the Gentiles in his plan of salvation. So Paul argued, "Can't you see that God is equally just in crediting the righteousness of one man, Jesus Christ, to the whole human race?" With these verses Paul is only expanding on what he wrote earlier: "There is no difference, for all have sinned and fall short of the glory of God, and are justified freely by his grace through the redemption that came by Christ Jesus" (3:22-24).

The thrust of Paul's whole argument in this context requires that we understand the whole human race to be the object of God's universal justice. God's condemnation of the whole race because of Adam's sin was just, and so also is God's justification of the whole race in Christ.

Now we can understand why Paul used the word *many* a couple times in this context. In both cases his emphasis is on the great number of all those affected by God's judgment as opposed to the limited number of Jews. That is especially clear in verse 15 of chapter 5, where he wrote, "For if the many died by the trespass of the one man, how much more did God's grace and the gift that came by the grace of the one man, Jesus Christ, overflow to the many!" When Paul said, "the many died," he certainly meant that all people died because of Adam's sin. So, in the second half of the verse, "the many" to whom the gift of Christ overflows must mean *all*.

In the Apostles' Creed, we confess, "I believe in the Holy Spirit . . . the forgiveness of sins." With this statement, week after week, we affirm our trust that objectively, in Christ, without and apart from our faith, God declares forgiveness to all. This creedal statement expresses belief in something that already exists by the merit of Christ and the decree of God. That is good news.

Who benefits from justification?

Through faith alone we benefit from justification.

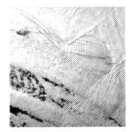

5

Who Benefits from Justification?

Faith receives God's justifying declaration of righteousness for sinners. Although God declares all to be free from sin through Jesus' blood and righteousness, only believers enjoy the benefit of justification, namely, the forgiveness of sins.

One justification

There is only one justification, the one God declared by grace, for Christ's sake, on Easter morning. But the Bible speaks of this one justification from two points of view. When the Bible says God objectively declared all to be righteous, we call that *objective justification*. When the Bible says the individual sinner subjectively believes and enjoys that forgiveness for himself, we call that *subjective justification*.

There are not, however, two different justifications. Nor should we think in terms of two different kinds of the same justification. There is only one justification of sinners, the one God declared for Jesus' sake on Easter morning. God does not justify the sinner anew when he comes to faith. The justification that at some point the individual comes to believe is the same justification God first declared for all sinners. We say that we are justified by faith alone because by faith alone do we come to trust and appreciate the righteousness God declared for all.

Subjective justification is what the Lutheran Confessions speak about when they emphasize justification by faith. Subjective justification means that we are the *subjects* who have received forgiveness; forgiveness becomes our personal possession. We own and enjoy peace with God.

Justification by faith

Faith is essentially trust, reliance, complete dependence, the resting of the heart on God. Simple trust receives what God gives. Paul wrote, "To the man who does not work but trusts God who justifies the wicked, his faith is credited as righteousness" (Romans 4:5). David's poetry reflects on the nature of this happy trust: "But I trust in your unfailing love; my heart rejoices in your salvation" (Psalm 13:5).

Faith is the reliance of the human heart, soul, and mind on divine grace. In the upper room, Jesus pleaded with his disciples, "Trust in God; trust also in me" (John 14:1). Isaiah invited his people to rely on the coming Savior: "See, I lay a stone in Zion, a tested stone, a precious cornerstone for a sure foundation; the one who trusts will never be dismayed" (Isaiah 28:16). John wrote, "So we know and rely on the love God has for us" (1 John 4:16).

So, while the essential nature of saving faith is trust, the function of faith is that of a receptor. Faith is a receiving hand that accepts God's justifying grace. Since faith is simple trust created in us by the gracious working of God, the only function faith can have is to receive what God offers.

The power of faith

The great power of faith, however, lies neither in its nature nor in its function. Faith does not justify us because it receives something. The object of faith—what we receive—justifies us. In other words, faith does not save us; what faith lays hold of saves us. That's why it is more proper to say that we are saved *through* faith than to say that we are saved *by* faith. The benefit of faith is not the strength of our trust but the magnitude of God's gift. Every sinner that God leads to faith is justified and receives all the blessings of forgiveness. That is equally true whether faith is very strong or very weak.

Justification by faith alone

When Lutherans insist that faith alone justifies, we mean that good works do not contribute to our salvation. Salvation is one hundred percent faith in Christ and zero percent good works. Numerous Bible passages unequivocally exclude good works in connection with justification. Paul said, "He [God] saved us, not because of righteous things we had done, but because of his mercy" (Titus 3:5). "We . . . know that a man is not justified by observing the law, but by faith in Jesus Christ" (Galatians 2:15,16). When Lutherans insist that faith alone justifies, we also mean that our faith itself is not a meritorious act. We mean that we are not contributing to our salvation in any way by the act of believing. Our believing neither earns nor intentionally receives God's forgiveness. Faith is a gift from God, just like the salvation faith receives.

So we must not think of our faith as a moral act of obedience to the law. Faith has nothing to do with the law. The apostle boldly confessed to the Galatians, "So we, too, have put our faith in Christ Jesus that we may be justified by faith in Christ and not by observing the law, because by observing the law no one will be justified (Galatians 2:16).

For Luther, the clearest Scripture on this matter was Romans 3:28: "We maintain that a man is justified by faith apart from observing the law." In his German translation of this verse, Luther added the word *alone* in connection with *faith* to bring out the emphasis of the text. Luther was criticized for adding a word to the translation, but he stood his ground. He wrote:

> Note, then, whether Paul does not assert more vehemently that faith alone justifies than I do, although he does not use the word 'alone,' which I have used. For he who says: Works do not justify, but faith justifies, certainly affirms more strongly that faith justifies than does he who says: Faith alone justifies.[21]

Paul put the same thought into other words: "However, to the man who does not work but trusts God who justifies the wicked, his faith is credited as righteousness" (Romans 4:5). Here the apostle repeated the argument of chapter 3, verse 28, by saying that the "man who does not work" is justified. But he made an additional point about faith when he said that "God . . . justifies the wicked." God gave us the faith to receive his justification while we were still considered morally wicked. Neither our life prior to conversion nor faith itself makes us worthy of God's righteous decree.

The decisive argument of Scripture against the human merit of faith is its clear teaching of objective justification (see chapter 4). God's "innocent" verdict for all was proclaimed prior to and apart from any sinner's acceptance of it by faith. Our faith is not a condition that we have to meet in order to be forgiven. God justified the sinner while he was still sinful and without faith, and God says so in the gospel. Faith does not bring about forgiveness. It merely lays hold of a forgiveness that already existed. Our prayers for forgiveness do not cause God to forgive us; they are merely an expression of our faith that he already has.

God creates saving faith in us

Faith takes place within our hearts and minds, but we do not create or perpetuate our own faith. An analogy might help. Dinner is made in the kitchen, but the kitchen does not make the dinner. There must always be a cook. In a similar way, Scripture insists that, even though faith happens in our hearts, it is God who makes it happen there. Every Lutheran confirmand memorizes Ephesians 2:8,9: "For it is by grace you have been saved, through faith—and this not from yourselves, it is the gift of God—not by works, so that no one can boast."

God's Holy Spirit creates saving faith in us. He enters our hearts and minds through his message of the gospel and creates trust there. God converts our sinful minds that are by nature hostile to him (Romans 8:7) and opens them to accept his saving declaration of forgiveness. That was certainly Luther's understanding when he wrote the opening words of his explanation to the Third Article of the Apostles' Creed in the Small Catechism: "I cannot by my own thinking or choosing believe in Jesus Christ, my Lord, or come to him. But the Holy Spirit has called me by the gospel."

God always takes the initiative to create faith in us by his Spirit, using the Word and the Sacrament of Baptism. Paul reminded the Ephesians, "You also were included in Christ when you heard the word of truth, the gospel of your salvation" (Ephesians 1:13). To the Corinthians who benefited from the Spirit's prompting work, Paul said, "No one can say, 'Jesus is Lord,' except by the Holy Spirit" (1 Corinthians 12:3). There is no other way that sinners are led to trust what God has done for our salvation. "'No eye has seen, no ear has heard, no mind has conceived what God has prepared for those who love him'—but God has revealed it to us by his Spirit" (1 Corinthians 2:9,10). By grace alone God does the work to create faith in us. Jesus told his disciples, "You did not choose me, but I chose you and appointed you to go and bear fruit" (John 15:16).

Faith alone is subverted

The faith that receives justification is faith alone. It's as simple as that. But in the history of Christianity, as well as in modern America, many movements have tried to complicate simple saving faith by mixing it with or replacing it with human effort.

In February of 1997, the Lutheran World Federation (LWF) released the Joint Declaration on the Doctrine of Justification (JDDJ), a statement developed jointly by Lutheran and Roman Catholic representatives. The many Lutherans who were offended and confused by this much-publicized document should know that not all Lutherans participated in formulating it. The Lutherans who sat at the table with representatives from the Vatican were members of the Lutheran World Federation. The LWF is an international group of Lutheran churches that are on record as opposing the inerrancy of the Scriptures, the six-day creation, and even Christ's physical resurrection from the dead. It should not surprise us that they found common ground with Roman Catholic theologians. Actually, the Joint Declaration was not an agreement in the usual sense of the word. It was a mutual arrangement to publicly accept the unresolvable disagreements between Lutherans and Roman Catholics.

The Joint Declaration calls into question the nature of faith as taught by Scripture and proclaimed by the reformers. Three glaring differences between historic Lutheranism and Roman Catholicism were not resolved. First, Rome refused to concede its long-time insistence that faith does not stand alone. The Vatican maintained that a sinner's loving response to what it calls God's infused grace precedes God's justification through faith. In other words, first God gives a person a little starter shot of love, then the person responds with acceptance and conviction, and finally God, for the sake of that response, forgives the person.

The Lutherans who participated in the Joint Declaration allowed Rome's insistence on infused grace to stand alongside their own definition of faith alone. They knew full well that by *grace* Rome meant a spiritual power poured into the soul to enable a person to merit salvation. Lutherans, by contrast, understand grace as God's merciful disposition toward us. Yet the LWF publicly declared that the different ways of expressing the truth about the role of faith should not stand in the way of dialogue between the churches. These are its own words: "Therefore the Lutheran and Catholic explications of justification are in their difference open to one another and do not destroy the consensus regarding basic truths" (JDDJ 40).

Second, Rome also refused to concede that justification by faith was the central teaching of Scripture—the teaching by which all other doctrines of the church should be judged. The Lutherans offered such wording, but the Vatican vetoed it and inserted its own wording. It agreed to acknowledge justification by faith as *one of a number* of indispensable criteria (JDDJ 18).

A third fault of the proposed agreement is that it hedges on the basic meaning of justification. Traditional Roman Catholicism has always taught a transforming view of justification. It considers justification to be a gradual moral change in an individual believer. For Roman Catholics, justification is a process, not a proclamation. And they did not back down from this position in the Joint Declaration. They refused to accept the Bible's own teaching of justification by faith as an instantaneous act of God that immediately confers all the grace of forgiveness. Rome still does not accept grace alone, Christ alone, or faith alone, according to the biblical use of these terms. This is the fatal flaw of the Joint Declaration. It renders the careful wording of the document to be mere deception.

Another present-day challenge to the Bible's teaching of faith alone is the decision theology so prominent in many Evangelical and Reformed churches. The call to "make your decision for Christ" is harmful for two reasons. First, it falsely ascribes to sinners the ability to make the right decision. Second, it robs God of his converting grace by crediting us for participating in it.

Because many Evangelicals emphasize the Bible and historic Christian faith, they sometimes cannot understand why Lutherans make such a big fuss about their teaching on conversion. But when you listen carefully to the difference between a Baptist and a Lutheran missionary's message, the matter becomes clear. A Baptist missionary will say, "If you believe, you will be forgiven." A Lutheran will say, "You have been forgiven; believe it!" This is not a minor difference. For the Baptist, justification is conditional; it depends on the person's decision. To the Lutheran, justification is God's unconditional proclamation and faith's only role is passive, to believe and receive.

Another more subtle challenge to justifying faith is the increasingly skewed notion of faith held by the modern world. In our pluralistic society, the public media extol the virtues of personal faith and what they call faith traditions. They cannot be caught promoting any particular religion, so they devote all their reporting to the strength of faith and make little or no mention of the object of faith. This persistent media approach popularizes the notion that it makes no difference what you believe, as long as you have faith in something.

But such attention to faith damns it with faint praise. The value of our faith before God is not what we put into it but what we get out of it. We are justified not by how strongly we believe but by the strength of what we believe in. Not the determination and grit of the human spirit but the object of faith is all-important. Faith in false gods, faith in our ability to conquer cancer, faith that we will win the ball game—or faith in Santa Claus for that matter—is not saving faith. Jesus will put you at his right side at the final judgment, not because you had faith but because your faith rested in him.

Justification is a clear biblical message

Only the Bible's clear announcement of justification through faith alone can stand against the many voices Satan sends out to oppose it. Saving faith is not a human decision; it is not an infused ability to gradually wend our way into God's favor. And, no matter how intense our faith is, believing in the wrong thing is only faith in ourselves and not in Christ. The Word proclaims justification to be an objective, historical reality, apart from and before our faith. It is true whether or not we believe it. So when we believe, what the Holy Spirit has created in us is simple trust in real good news.

One of our hymns aptly expresses the gospel's appeal to the troubled sinner's heart:

> Riven the rock for me,
> Thirst to relieve,
> Manna from heaven falls
> Fresh ev'ry eve.
> Never a want severe
> Causeth my eye a tear,
> But thou dost whisper near,
> "Only believe." (CW 473:2)

Luther's "faith alone" theme runs through his catechetical teachings. In his exposition of the Sacrament of Holy Baptism, he wrote, "It is certainly not the water that does such things, but God's Word which is in and with the water and faith which trusts this Word used with the water." Again, in regard to Holy Communion, Luther wrote, "Fasting and other outward preparations may serve a good purpose, but he is properly prepared who believes these words, 'Given' and 'poured out for you for the forgiveness of sins.'"

Justification "by faith alone" is also highlighted in the Lutheran confessional writings. The Augsburg Confession of 1530 in a memorable way summarizes the Lutheran teaching on justification with four prepositional phrases. Justification is "by grace, for Christ's sake, through faith" and not "by our own merits, works, or satisfactions."[22]

God's proclamation that the sinner has been declared righteous in Christ is both the invitation to the sinner and the power to accept that invitation. In the letter to the Romans, where Paul so beautifully preaches justification by faith, he wrote in the opening verses: "I am not ashamed of the gospel, because it is the power of God for the salvation of everyone who believes. . . . For in the gospel a righteousness from God is revealed, a righteousness that is by faith from first to last, just as it is written: 'The righteous will live by faith'" (verses 16,17).

How long does it take to be justified?

Believers receive full forgiveness instantly.

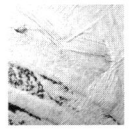

6

How Long Does It Take to Be Justified?

Instant forgiveness

Justification by faith is not a process. It happens instantaneously. There is no middle ground between having faith and not having faith. Jesus stated this truth in simple fashion to Nicodemus: "Whoever believes in him is not condemned, but whoever does not believe stands condemned already because he has not believed in the name of God's one and only Son" (John 3:18).

It is all right for us to talk about somebody's journey to faith taking place over a period of time. Coming to faith includes the Holy Spirit's work on the heart to convict it of sin as well as the message of God's grace in Christ. So the process of coming to faith may last for days, even years. But at any moment during that time, the individual sinner is either a believer or an unbeliever. Either he enjoys forgiveness or he rejects forgiveness. At any instant every person is under God's grace or wrath, headed for heaven or hell.

Jesus applied this principle to the idolatry of money. "No one can serve two masters," he said. "Either he will hate the one and love the other, or he will be devoted to the one and despise the other. You cannot serve both God and Money" (Matthew 6:24). In the Great Commission he again stated the matter unequivocally: "Whoever believes and is baptized will be saved, but whoever does not believe will be condemned" (Mark 16:16). We may say that a person has weak faith, but at no time is a person half believer and half unbeliever.

Full forgiveness

Either we have faith or we do not have faith. That, of course, does not rule out the variations between weak faith and strong faith. Jesus commended the faith of the centurion: "I tell you the truth, I have not found anyone in Israel with such great faith" (Matthew 8:10). He did the same with the Canaanite woman: "Woman, you have great faith! Your request is granted" (Matthew 15:28). But he warned the Laodiceans that their weak faith put them in danger of losing their faith completely: "Because you are lukewarm—neither hot nor cold—I am about to spit you out of my mouth" (Revelation 3:16).

According to God's promise, it is the presence of faith—not the strength or weakness of it—that grasps God's justifying decree. Thus the sinner with weak faith receives the same blessing of forgiveness as the one with strong faith. The problem with weak faith is not that it does not possess all the enjoyment of justification but that it stands in constant peril of being lost. That is why it is good for the prayer of the father of the boy with an evil spirit to be on the lips of every Christian: "I do believe; help me overcome my unbelief" (Mark 9:24).

No one would attest that the faith of the dying criminal on the cross was well developed in knowledge or strength. Yet Jesus promised him the full benefit of justifying faith: "I tell you the truth, today you will be with me in paradise" (Luke 23:43).

The problems with gradualism

Problems arise when people think of justification by faith as a gradual process. We might treat those with weak faith as though they are only partially forgiven or as though they do not have faith at all. This might lead us to deprive them of the very comfort of the full gospel that would strengthen their faith.

Typical of this problem is the complicated system of masses, penances, and saint worship within the Roman Catholic Church. Rome formally teaches and defends the teaching of gradual justification. This creates doubt in a believer's mind about what his status with God is at any time. This doubt, in turn, makes one dependent upon the ritual requirements of the church. Recall that the Reformation was sparked by Luther's disgust with Rome's selling of indulgences. These indulgences promoted the false idea that the visible church dispenses forgiveness in bits and pieces. Luther insisted that the church was to proclaim God's full and free forgiveness to the sinner, not dole it out a little at a time.

Another problem with gradualism is its suggestion that there are levels of Christianity. This false teaching breeds caste systems in the church, such as *water-baptized* and *Spirit-baptized* Christians. Some of the Corinthians who spoke in tongues looked down on those who did not have that same gift, and Paul chastised them for it (1 Corinthians 12). What we give to God in good works may reflect the strength of our faith and personal gifts. But the amount of our good works does not determine that which God has given to every believer: full and free forgiveness in justification for Christ's sake.

Another problem of viewing justification by faith as a process is that it inevitably invites the thought that we participate in bringing ourselves to faith. We wrote at length in the last chapter how God's Holy Word specifically rules out any effort or cooperation on our part in faith. When we are struggling to give up sins and seeking to come closer to God, we are not in the process of coming to faith; we are already justified and are acting on the Spirit's power of faith in us. That was how Paul urged Timothy to grow in the faith he already had: "For this reason I remind you to fan into flame the gift of God, which is in you through the laying on of my hands" (2 Timothy 1:6).

Solid comfort

The nature of Christian life is to enjoy and give thanks for what we have in justification. The last thing we need to worry about when our faith is weak is whether we have been fully forgiven. The Spirit strengthens our weak faith in the same way that he created it in the first place. He assures us that, in spite of our doubts, God has removed all our guilt and punishment by ascribing to us Jesus' perfect life and atoning death. The book of Romans reveals that the faith of the Roman Christians was less than perfect, yet Paul assured all of them that they possessed the full benefit of justification. He wrote, "Therefore, since we have been justified through faith, we have peace with God through our Lord Jesus Christ" (Romans 5:1).

Paul went on to explain that every believer, regardless of his strength of faith, lives in what Lutheran teachers have called a *state of grace*. "Through [Jesus]," Paul said, "we have gained access by faith into this grace in which we now stand" (Romans 5:2).

Although weak faith puts us in greater danger of losing our faith completely, the Savior who earned our justification does not reject us on account of our weak faith. Our Lord fulfilled the messianic prophesy about himself by dealing gently with those with wavering faith. Matthew wrote about Jesus, "A bruised reed he will not break, and a smoldering wick he will not snuff out" (Matthew 12:20). Jesus strengthened faith with the same assurance by which he created it. "When Jesus saw their faith, he said to the paralytic, 'Take heart, son; your sins are forgiven'" (Matthew 9:2).

The false teaching that we have not been fully forgiven, or that we will be gradually forgiven and must add our own effort to God's grace, is a heavy yoke on the troubled sinner. The motivation for moral living becomes an attempt to appease a God who is still not completely satisfied with us. The joy of living in thanksgiving is stifled or killed. This mode of existence differs little from pagan sacrifices. It is a natural human religious attitude that seeks to win a way to God through personal effort.

Paul addressed this tendency that even Christians have to revert to a man-made approach to God. He encouraged the Galatians, "It is for freedom that Christ has set us free. Stand firm, then, and do not let yourselves be burdened again by a yoke of slavery" (Galatians 5:1). Paul's urging is especially appropriate for Lutherans who may take for granted the precious heritage of spiritual freedom won by Luther and the reformers. Let us rise each new day with the faith that justification is certain, instantaneous, and complete. And when doubts seek to enslave our weakening faith, let us seek new strength, not in our own efforts but in the completed work of our Savior.

What also happens when we are justified?

God also enables us
to live holy lives.

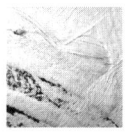

7

What Also Happens When We Are Justified?

Sanctification

At the same moment that we are justified through faith, God begins another work in us. This work is called sanctification. Sanctification means the work of making somebody or something holy. To sanctify means to consecrate, that is, to set apart for God's exclusive use. That sense of the word is evident in Paul's words to Timothy: "If a man cleanses himself from the latter [ignoble purposes], he will be an instrument for noble purposes, made holy [sanctified], useful to the Master and prepared to do any good work" (2 Timothy 2:21).

The Bible generally speaks of sanctification as the work of the Holy Spirit. The Holy Spirit consecrates the justified to do good works for God. Paul wrote to the Romans that he was a minister to the Gentiles, "so that the Gentiles might become an offering acceptable to God, sanctified by the Holy Spirit" (Romans 15:16). In the Small Catechism, Luther also assigned the work of sanctification to the Holy Spirit in his explanation of the Third Article of the Apostles' Creed: "The Holy Spirit has called me by the gospel, enlightened me with his gifts, sanctified and kept me in the true faith."

Not every mention of sanctification in the Bible, however, refers to this specific work of setting believers apart for good works to God. Because *sanctification* means to set somebody apart for God, the word is sometimes used as a synonym for *justification*. That seems to be the meaning, for instance, in 1 Corinthians 6:11: "You were washed, you were sanctified, you were justified in the name of the Lord Jesus Christ and by the Spirit of our God." This also seems to be the sense of the word in Ephesians 5:25,26: "Christ loved the church and gave himself up for her to make her holy [sanctify her], cleansing her by the washing with water through the word."

Sanctification is a work in progress

Our justification is complete the moment we are brought to faith. Sanctification begins at that same instant, but the work of the Spirit to make us holy is an ongoing process. It continues in us until the day we die. Justification immediately and completely changes our status before God. We are declared to be holy in his sight for Christ's sake. Sanctification is the Spirit's effort to change our personal moral quality. Our personal moral change is always incomplete and continues until we die.

The various wrongheaded ideas out there about justification and sanctification are evidence that many people find the difference between those terms difficult to understand. That is because both of them deal with holiness. In justification God declares us to be holy. In sanctification God gradually leads us to live holy lives. Yet, because the Scriptures make a clear distinction, we know that it is important for our faith to understand that distinction.

Note how the writer to the Hebrews included both justification and sanctification in the same thought: "By one sacrifice he has made perfect forever those who are being made holy" (Hebrews 10:14). Justification is a completed act in the mind of this inspired writer. He says that Jesus "has made" us perfect. Yet God's work among us "who are being made holy" is an ongoing effort.

The same distinction can be seen in Paul's letter to the Philippians. First he wrote that he has already been declared holy, or righteous, through faith in Christ: "I consider them [all things] rubbish that I may gain Christ and be found in him, not having a righteousness of my own that comes from the law, but that which is through faith in Christ—the righteousness that comes from God and is by faith" (Philippians 3:8,9). Then, just a breath later, he added, "Not that I have already obtained all this, or have already been made perfect, but I press on to take hold of that for which Christ Jesus took hold of me" (3:12). Paul was confident that he had already been declared holy in justification through faith, but he admitted that he had not yet been made perfect in sanctification.

So, while you and I take comfort that in justification Jesus has already taken hold of us, we wrestle with taking hold of Jesus in holy living. In order to help us in this ongoing struggle, Jesus sends us spiritual servants in the church to promote this process. He gives us pastors and teachers "to prepare God's people for works of service, so that the body of Christ may be built up until we all reach unity in the faith and in the knowledge of the Son of God and become mature, attaining to the whole measure of the fullness of Christ" (Ephesians 4:12,13).

Sanctification begins with the creation of a new self

The work of sanctification is initiated by the Holy Spirit. At the same time that he leads us to trust God's justifying love, he creates in each of us a "new self." With the creation of the new self in us, the holy image of God, which was lost in the fall into sin, is being restored in us.

God's image, of course, is not a physical image but a spiritual one. It includes perfect knowledge of God and his will. Paul told the Colossians: "You have taken off your old self with its practices and have put on the new self, which is being renewed in knowledge in the image of its Creator" (Colossians 3:9,10). The new self is holy like God himself, so it desires only what God wants. "You were taught, with regard to your former way of life, to put off your old self, which is being corrupted by its deceitful desires; to be made new in the attitude of your minds; and to put on the new self, created to be like God in true righteousness and holiness" (Ephesians 4:22-24).

The new self created in us by the Holy Spirit returns to the believer the ability lost in the Fall. Through the gift of the new self, you and I are now able to do the will of God from the heart. "For the grace of God that brings salvation has appeared to all men. It teaches us to say 'No' to ungodliness and worldly passions, and to live self-controlled, upright and godly lives in this present age" (Titus 2:11,12).

The new self desires the things of God. "Do not conform any longer to the pattern of this world, but be transformed by the renewing of your mind. Then you will be able to test and approve what God's will is—his good, pleasing and perfect will" (Romans 12:2).

Many object to the Bible's clear message of justification by faith because, they say, it provides an excuse for sinful living. If people may know for sure that—no matter how they live—all their sins are freely and fully forgiven, they will go and live however they want—or so the argument goes. Some of Luther's opponents during the Reformation argued that way. They felt that people needed to carry around some guilt and doubt to motivate them for right living.

Already in his day, Paul was forced to address this same objection to the teaching of justification. After preaching justification through faith for three chapters in his letter to the Romans (chapters 3–5), Paul anticipated this objection: "What shall we say, then? Shall we go on sinning so that grace may increase?" (Romans 6:1). He knew what his detractors were thinking: Preaching free grace through justification would only make people sin more so that they could be forgiven more.

Paul answered these objections by tying justification directly to sanctification: "For we know that our old self was crucified with him so that the body of sin might be done away with, that we should no longer be slaves to sin—because anyone who has died has been freed from sin" (Romans 6:6,7).

One favorite Lutheran hymn makes the same connection. Jesus, our Rock of ages, not only cleanses us from the guilt of our sins in justification, he sanctifies us to break the power of sin in our lives:

> Rock of Ages, cleft for me,
> Let me hide myself in thee;
> Let the water and the blood
> From thy riven side which flowed
> Be of sin the double cure:
> Cleanse me from its guilt and pow'r. (CW 389:1)

Jesus' work on the cross is the basis of both justification and sanctification. The two cannot be separated. Justification cleanses us from the guilt of our sin while, at the same time, sanctification cleanses us from the power of sin. Since the Holy Spirit has created the new self in us, sin no longer has the power to dominate our thoughts and actions. Paul concurs: "Now that you have been set free from sin and have become slaves to God, the benefit you reap leads to holiness" (Romans 6:22).

Sanctification is a cooperative effort

In earlier chapters we went to great lengths to show from Scripture that justification is a unilateral action of a gracious God. In eternity the Father loved us and planned our salvation. The Son entered this world, fully human, and by his perfect life, his atoning death, and his triumphant resurrection secured for us God's declaration of "Not guilty!" By his own effort, without our cooperation, the Holy Spirit led us to reach out and grasp justification by faith. Justification is by grace alone, by Christ alone, through faith alone.

Sanctification also begins with God's power. The Holy Spirit initiated our sanctification when he created a new self in us. But the Bible speaks of our growth in holiness as a cooperative work between the Holy Spirit and us. Since God has given us a new self, we have something on the inside that willingly works along with the Holy Spirit in doing good works. Our church fathers have suggested that this cooperative work is like the yoking of an ant to an elephant. We are the ant, of course. Yet God stoops to include us in this finishing work of salvation and call us his coworkers.

The Bible says that we are partners with God in our efforts to serve him with a holy life. Paul wrote, "Therefore, my dear friends, as you have always obeyed—not only in my presence, but now much more in my absence—continue to work out your salvation with fear and trembling, for it is God who works in you to will and to act according to his good purpose" (Philippians 2:12,13).

While faith and forgiveness are "not by works, so that no one can boast," Paul added, "We are God's workmanship, created in Christ Jesus to do good works, which God prepared in advance for us to do" (Ephesians 2:9,10). This passage beautifully illustrates the relationship between God and believers in doing good works. We ourselves do the good works. But note that we are God's workmanship. Our new self was created in Christ Jesus, and God planned our opportunities for service in advance. Our contribution is the result of God's grace and power. So God still receives all the credit for our sanctification.

Sanctification is thanksgiving

The life of the justified sinner is characterized above all by thanksgiving. Sanctification is the Spirit's power in us through the new self to say thanks for justification in everything we do. Christians are mindful of God's mercy, and they willingly offers their entire lives to God as thank-offerings. "Therefore, I urge you, brothers, in view of God's mercy, to offer your bodies as living sacrifices, holy and pleasing to God—this is your spiritual act of worship"

(Romans 12:1). When we think about what Christ has done for us, we want to imitate God and live lives of love. "Be imitators of God, therefore, as dearly loved children and live a life of love, just as Christ loved us and gave himself up for us as a fragrant offering and sacrifice to God" (Ephesians 5:1,2).

The sanctified believer's life exudes praise. Paul's words encourage us: "Sing and make music in your heart to the Lord, always giving thanks to God the Father for everything, in the name of our Lord Jesus Christ" (Ephesians 5:19,20). "And whatever you do, whether in word or deed, do it all in the name of the Lord Jesus, giving thanks to God the Father through him" (Colossians 3:17). "Be joyful always; pray continually; give thanks in all circumstances, for this is God's will for you in Christ Jesus" (1 Thessalonians 5:16-18).

The full and sure forgiveness granted in justification by faith makes the full and free thanksgiving of sanctified life possible. The new self offers willing, not grudging, obedience to God. We are not bound by guilt to obey. We are not compelled by lingering doubts to earn our way to heaven. Everything we offer to God comes without compulsion. That is the most sincere form of thanks.

The struggle between the new self and the sinful flesh

The ideal Christian life is a life of peace with God. No guilt. No doubt. Willing obedience. Overflowing thanksgiving. All gifts of God. But believers must also deal with the real. And the reality is that we still have our sinful flesh clinging to us. "I know that nothing good lives in me, that is, in my sinful nature," Paul confessed in Romans 7:18. The reality in this sinful world is that we are at the same time both saints and sinners—justified, yet struggling with our sanctification.

The same apostle who so often wrote about Christian joy and thanksgiving was also forced to admit this terrible struggle within himself. Paul wrote, "I have the desire to do what is good, but I cannot carry it out. For what I do is not the good I want to do; no, the evil I do not want to do—this I keep on doing" (Romans 7:18,19).

Our struggle of the new self to dominate the sinful nature is the good fight, the fight of faith. We call it the good fight because only the believer has the ability to fight it. Only the believer in whom the Spirit has created the new self in God's image constantly wrestles for dominance against the old man, the sinful flesh. We win some; we lose some. But, led by the Spirit, we are dissatisfied that we do not win more. Paul described his personal anguish:

> So I find this law at work: When I want to do good, evil is right there with me. For in my inner being I delight in God's law; but I see another law at work in the members of my body, waging war against the law of my mind and making me a prisoner of the law of sin at work within my members. What a wretched man I am! Who will rescue me from this body of death? (Romans 7:21-24)

Growth in sanctification

As vicious as the struggle of the new self against the old is, we are never left to stand alone on the field of battle. Paul answered his own question of despair: "Who will rescue me from this body of death? Thanks be to God—through Jesus Christ our Lord!" (Romans 7:24,25). Jesus, who threw us into this battle by redeeming us from the unbelieving world, gives us everything we need to conquer in the strife.

Paul was talking about the battle of sanctification when he wrote to the Ephesians:

> Finally, be strong in the Lord and in his mighty power. Put on the full armor of God so that you can take your stand against the devil's schemes. For our struggle is not against flesh and blood, but against the rulers, against the authorities, against the powers of this dark world and against the spiritual forces of evil in the heavenly realms. Therefore put on the full armor of God, so that when the day of evil comes, you may be able to stand your ground. (Ephesians 6:10-13)

Even the best soldiers can run out of ammunition. Even the strongest Christians can expend their defensive resources fighting the sanctification battles of this life. Our whole life of sanctification, then, is one of rearming. Our growth in Bible knowledge results in our growth of faith and works. Paul encouraged the Philippians to grow: "This is my prayer: that your love may abound more and more in knowledge and depth of insight, so that you may be able to discern what is best and may be pure and blameless until the day of Christ, filled with the fruit of righteousness that comes through Jesus Christ—to the glory and praise of God" (Philippians 1:9-11).

While we rejoice in the status of saints imparted to us in justification, the Holy Spirit sanctifies us with a dissatisfaction with our personal imperfection. The same forgiveness that remits the sins of the past moves us to forsake those sins in the future. Paul explained:

> Not that I have already obtained all this, or have already been made perfect, but I press on to take hold of that for which Christ Jesus took hold of me. Brothers, I do not consider myself yet to have taken hold of it. But one thing I do: Forgetting what is behind and straining toward what

is ahead, I press on toward the goal to win the prize for which God has called me heavenward in Christ Jesus. (Philippians 3:12-14)

Christ's love for us compels our love for him. Our love for him urges us to know more about him. "Therefore let us leave the elementary teachings about Christ and go on to maturity, not laying again the foundation of repentance from acts that lead to death, and of faith in God" (Hebrews 6:1). Growth in sanctification means that we do not rest on our laurels. Satisfaction with our level of sanctification is evidence of weak faith. It can lead us to self-righteousness and move us to lay down our weapons in the good fight of faith.

The sanctified believer wants to avoid the confirmation syndrome, the idea that we learned enough as adolescents to fight all of our mature battles. "We want each of you to show this same diligence to the very end, in order to make your hope sure. We do not want you to become lazy, but to imitate those who through faith and patience inherit what has been promised" (Hebrews 6:11,12).

The Holy Spirit equips us for battles in sanctification by the same means he used to bring us to faith in justification. Those means are the gospel in the Word and in the sacraments. Scripture knowledge that comes from personal Bible reading, family devotions, worship attendance, and Bible study builds our faith and rearms our defenses. If we rely on basic teachings learned years ago, our growth in sanctification is stunted, and we won't shine like lights in the world.

> In fact, though by this time you should be teachers, you need someone to teach you the elementary truths of God's word all over again. You need milk, not solid food! Any-

one who lives on milk, being still an infant, is not acquainted with the teaching about righteousness. But solid food is for the mature, who by constant use have trained themselves to distinguish good from evil. (Hebrews 5:12-14)

Paul also used the picture of little babies living on milk to describe Christians who are immature in their understanding and their lives of good works. Paul rebuked the Corinthians: "I could not address you as spiritual but as worldly—mere infants in Christ. I gave you milk, not solid food, for you were not yet ready for it. Indeed, you are still not ready. You are still worldly. For since there is jealousy and quarreling among you, are you not worldly?" (1 Corinthians 3:1-3). In Ephesians Paul added that we should continue growing in our sanctification "until we all reach unity in the faith and in the knowledge of the Son of God and become mature, attaining to the whole measure of the fullness of Christ. Then we will no longer be infants" (Ephesians 4:13,14).

Our church leaders, especially, must grow spiritually in the Word. Deacons, Paul wrote, "must keep hold of the deep truths of the faith with a clear conscience" (1 Timothy 3:9). Pastors and elders receive similar encouragement: "Be diligent in these matters; give yourself wholly to them, so that everyone may see your progress. Watch your life and doctrine closely. Persevere in them, because if you do, you will save both yourself and your hearers" (1 Timothy 4:15,16). Even those aspiring to what we might think to be lesser offices in the church need to be full of the Spirit's Word. When the apostles chose men to wait on tables in Jerusalem, they looked for men who were "known to be full of the Spirit and wisdom" (Acts 6:3).

Sanctification is never complete in this life

Although we constantly grow in faith and good works, we must humbly admit that we will never achieve perfection in this life. Scripture is unmistakably clear on the matter of personal perfection: "If we claim to be without sin, we deceive ourselves and the truth is not in us. If we claim we have not sinned, we make him out to be a liar and his word has no place in our lives" (1 John 1:8,10). "There is no one righteous, not even one; there is no one who understands, no one who seeks God. All have turned away, they have together become worthless; there is no one who does good, not even one" (Romans 3:10-12). "There is no difference, for all have sinned and fall short of the glory of God" (Romans 3:22,23).

The notion that we can eventually grow to perfection in this life is the official teaching in a number of so-called Holiness denominations. This false claim to perfection hurts the believer's relationship to God. First, as Saint John said, it makes God out to be a liar. God says that, although it is the goal of every believer to achieve the perfection of Jesus Christ, we will never achieve it here on earth.

Perfectionism also hurts our relationship with God because it depreciates the sanctifying work of the Spirit. Every word of Scripture that urges us to continue to grow is set aside by perfectionism. Strangely, many of the same churches that give a high profile to the Holy Spirit are the ones whose teaching of perfectionism despises his work of sanctification.

A third and fatal weakness of perfectionism is that it promotes self-righteousness. If we believe that we are already perfect, we will feel no need for the redeeming work of Jesus Christ and the teaching of justification. It is not surprising that perfectionist, or Holiness, church bodies downplay the sacraments of Baptism and the Lord's Supper. If you feel you do not need to be forgiven by God, then the forgiveness God offers and gives in the sacraments will be of little value.

Humility is one of the gifts we receive through the Spirit's work of sanctification. The humbleness of heart engendered in us through sanctification leads us to appreciate our justification all the more. When we come home after another day of battles with the devil, the world, and our own sinful flesh, we bow before the cross. Although our new selves have fought the good fight, we have lost some battles. We have come home bloodied from our losses, that is, our sins, and we beg to be washed clean again in the blood of our Savior. Full of sin and nearly out of ammunition, we ask to be restored, knowing full well that God in Christ has already declared us righteous.

At the same time that we are renewed in justification, God again gives us the Holy Spirit, who strengthens our new self in God's image. Now we are ready to go out and face life again. We accept Paul's urging: "Finally, brothers, we instructed you how to live in order to please God, as in fact you are living. Now we ask you and urge you in the Lord Jesus to do this more and more. . . . It is God's will that you should be sanctified. . . . For God did not call us to be impure, but to live a holy life" (1 Thessalonians 4:1,3,7).

What do our good works have to do with justification?

Our lives demonstrate
the justifying faith
in our hearts.

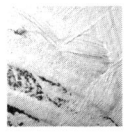

8

What Do Our Good Works Have to Do with Justification?

Invisible justification

Justification by Christ alone, by grace alone, through faith alone, is invisible. It was declared in the heart of God, and it is received through faith in the heart of the believer. Although openly proclaimed in the gospel of Scripture, justification through faith is unseen by the world. Even Christians cannot see the presence of justification in one another's hearts. Only God knows those who are his (Luke 16:15; 2 Timothy 2:19). Paul told the Colossians, "Your life is now hidden with Christ in God" (Colossians 3:3).

Visible justification

Holy Scripture also teaches a visible justification. Although our fellow Christians and the world around us cannot see our faith, they are able to see the fruits of our faith. The products of our faith, namely, our good works, testify to the presence of the invisible faith in our hearts. Thus, we are visibly justified by our works. Others regard us as righteous whenever good works show that we are believers.

Jesus talked about this visible justification. He told his disciples, "By this all men will know that you are my disciples, if you love one another" (John 13:35). He said, "Love your enemies and pray for those who persecute you, that you may be sons of your Father in heaven" (Matthew 5:44,45).

Our Lord also tied the evidence of good works to the final judgment. When the Pharisees accused him of being in league with the devil, Jesus said that he and all people will be justified by their actions:

> Make a tree good and its fruit will be good, or make a tree bad and its fruit will be bad, for a tree is recognized by its fruit. You brood of vipers, how can you who are evil say anything good? For out of the overflow of the heart the mouth speaks. The good man brings good things out of the good stored up in him, and the evil man brings evil things out of the evil stored up in him. But I tell you that men will have to give account on the day of judgment for every careless word they have spoken. For by your words you will be acquitted, and by your words you will be condemned. (Matthew 12:33-37)

Our Lord's parable about the sheep and goats at the final judgment is another case in point (Matthew 25:31-46). Jesus said those on his left will be people who did not serve him on earth. Those on his right hand will be those who provided food, water, clothing, and comfort to the needy in this life. The invisible faith in their hearts will be visibly proven by their works.

The apostles remind us that our good works prove our faith, not only to others but also to ourselves. When Peter told us "to make [our] calling and election sure" (2 Peter 1:10), he was urging us to produce the fruits of faith that are evidence to ourselves of the presence of faith in our hearts. John also spoke about how our good works are visible proof to ourselves of the saving faith in our hearts: "We know that we have come to know him if we obey his commands" (1 John 2:3). "We know that we have passed from death to life, because we love our brothers" (1 John 3:14).

Most notable among the apostles' writings on this subject are the words of James:

> What good is it, my brothers, if a man claims to have faith but has no deeds? Can such faith save him? Suppose a brother or sister is without clothes and daily food. If one of you says to him, "Go, I wish you well; keep warm and well fed," but does nothing about his physical needs, what good is it? In the same way, faith by itself, if it is not accompanied by action, is dead. (James 2:14-17)

What James wrote in his epistle confuses some people. James used exactly the same word for justification by works as Paul used for justification by faith. James wrote, "You see that a person is justified by what he does and not by faith alone" (2:24). When he wrote that a person is not justified by faith alone, he seemed to be directly contradicting what is clearly taught in the rest of Scriptures, especially in Paul's letters. Luther himself had trouble with this. Early in his ministry, he referred to the epistle of James as "an epistle of straw" and wondered out loud if the book belonged with the inspired writings of the New Testament. To Luther, James seemed to be undermining the heart of Reformation truth.

However, both the context of the letter and James' own words show that he is not opposing justification by faith alone. James wrote to the churches to combat what we might call an attitude of "dead orthodoxy." People were holding the truth of justification by faith, which Paul had written about earlier, but with false security they began to use the precious truth of full and free forgiveness as an excuse not to pursue moral living. In his opening words, James revealed the purpose of his writing when he urged his listeners, "Do not merely listen to the word, and so deceive yourselves. Do what it says" (1:22).

The manner in which members of the congregation were treating one another showed that James' audience had become lackadaisical in the pursuit of good works. They were neglecting the physical needs of the widows and orphans and openly discriminating against the poor. But with his own words, James clarified that when he speaks of justification by works he is talking about demonstrating faith in the heart—not about earning salvation. Justification by faith alone gains salvation. Justification by works shows the world that salvation has been gained. So James wrote, "I will show you my faith by what I do" (2:18). His closing comment on this matter leaves no doubt: "As the body without the spirit is dead, so faith without deeds is dead" (2:26). Faith alone saves; yet faith without good works is dead. Good works show that faith is alive.

No conflict in two justifications

The invisible justification by grace alone and the visible justification by works do not conflict with one another. These two justifications are not alternate or competing ways of gaining salvation. The fact that the Bible so often mentions visible justification by works does not set aside its clear message of invisible justification by faith alone. Good works are the evidence of faith and are done only by believers (Hebrews 11:6). Good works justify a person before others because they show that the person is a believer. Still, it is faith in Christ alone that gives us the perfect righteousness we need to enter heaven.

The church of all ages must teach justification by works. It may be that our present-day teachers neglect this teaching to some extent. There are, however, two compelling reasons for teaching justification by works just as we teach justification by faith. First and foremost is the fact that the Holy Spirit himself sets forth both teachings in the Scriptures.

Our clear teaching of justification by works will express our confidence that this teaching in no way sets aside justification through faith alone. By soft-pedaling justification by works, we may give rise to wrong impressions. For some, we may raise doubts about whether justification by works is compatible with justification through faith. From others, there may be the simple question of why we don't preach the whole will of God (Acts 20:27). Not to preach justification by works hints that the Scripture contradicts itself.

The other reason we want to proclaim justification by works is our trust that all Scripture is useful for teaching (2 Timothy 3:16). We can be sure that justification by works does not set aside justification through faith alone. In fact, the Spirit will use it to clarify and emphasize justification through faith alone. Not only will we ourselves better understand justification through faith alone; the unbelieving world that cannot see the justifying faith in our hearts will be led by our good works to note its presence. Our high morality reflects the power of the central truth of the Bible to those who do not read the Bible.

What is the current status of the justified?

We are saints, priests, children of God, and heirs.

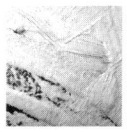

9

What Is the Current Status of the Justified?

The devil's chief ploy to undermine our Christian faith is accusation. He wants us to believe that either the size or the number or the frequency of our sins makes them unforgivable. In order to comfort us sinners when the devil accuses us, the holy writers of Scripture employed many different word pictures to assure us that we are indeed forgiven. Each of these words reminds us of the status before God enjoyed by those who are justified through faith.

Saints

One of the most commonly used words to describe the believers' status before God is *saints*. Literally *saints* means "holy ones." In the opening greeting of the letters that Paul sent to several congregations, he called the members of those churches saints: "To the saints in Ephesus, the faithful in Christ Jesus" (Ephesians 1:1), "To all the saints in Christ Jesus at Philippi" (Philippians 1:1), "To the church of God in Corinth, together with all the saints throughout Achaia" (2 Corinthians 1:1), "To all in Rome who are loved by God and called to be saints" (Romans 1:7).

What is notable about these congregations is that all of them contained sinners. In every one of his letters except one, Paul wrote to correct serious moral lapses and false teachings. Yet, remarkably, he called all the people in these churches saints. When he did not use the word *saint*, Paul used other similar phrases to describe the status of holiness that all his readers have in God's eyes through justification. In his first letter to the Corinthians, he wrote, "To the church of God in Corinth, to those sanctified in Christ Jesus and called to be holy, together with all those everywhere who call on the name of our Lord Jesus Christ—their Lord and ours" (1 Corinthians 1:2). Similarly he greeted the Colossians: "To the holy and faithful brothers in Christ at Colosse" (Colossians 1:2). Clearly, the word *saint* is used as a synonym for *believer*.

The Bible uses the word *saint* most often to refer to those who have been justified by faith in Christ Jesus and are now living in faith on earth. In a few places, the Bible refers to God's angels as holy ones (Jude 14), the same word used for saints. In a couple of references, those who have died in faith and are in heaven are called saints (Matthew 27:52, NIV "holy people"). But *saint* most commonly refers to believers who are still living on earth. A saint is one whom God has declared holy through justification.

The Roman Catholic Church, of course, uses the word *saint* in a way the Bible does not use it. Those who have proven themselves with a life of service and have performed some miracle may be declared by Rome to be saints. But we should recognize such saints as possessing merely a human title conferred by humans. It is for the joy and comfort of all Christians that God himself considers us saints and gives us that name in his Word. Our title was earned by Jesus, who led a perfect life on our behalf. His righteousness, his holiness, is credited to us in justification through faith.

Luther spoke at length about the assurance Christians receive from their status before God as saints:

> Just as we should not deny that we are baptized and are Christians, so we should not deny or doubt that we are holy. It would be good to impress this on the people well and to accustom them not to be frightened or scared by it. I and others, for example, were so deeply steeped in our monkery and unbelief that I was terrified by the thought that a man should consider himself holy on earth or let others call him holy. For our thoughts floated only up there among the deceased saints and blessed ones in heaven, even though in Scripture the word "holy" is always applied to those living here on earth. Thus St. Paul asks in nearly all his epistles that greetings be conveyed to the saints. He says: "All the saints greet you" (2 Cor. 13:13). And in 1 Tim. 5:10 he speaks of the widows who "washed the feet of the saints." Here he employed the word "saints" freely with reference to all Christians. And in the early Christian Church it was long customary for its members to call one another saints. This custom should still prevail. For it is not arrogant on the part of Christians to call one another holy because of Christ; it is glory and praise to God.[23]

To counter the accusations of Satan, Scripture connects many encouragements to our status as saints. Saints know that the Holy Spirit prays for them: "The Spirit intercedes for the saints in accordance with God's will"

(Romans 8:27). When our consciences accuse us: "He promises peace to his people, his saints" (Psalm 85:8). Saints do not worry that their eternal reward is in jeopardy: "I pray also that the eyes of your heart may be enlightened in order that you may know the hope to which he has called you, the riches of his glorious inheritance in the saints, and his incomparably great power for us who believe" (Ephesians 1:18,19).

Already now we can be confident that we will stand on the final day with our Savior: "Do you not know that the saints will judge the world?" (1 Corinthians 6:2). Because we are accredited by God as his holy ones, saints need never doubt the Father's love: "I pray that you, being rooted and established in love, may have power, together with all the saints, to grasp how wide and long and high and deep is the love of Christ" (Ephesians 3:17,18).

Wearers of white robes

Seven hundred years before Jesus came to earth, Isaiah spoke of the joy every believer in the Savior has through justification by faith: "I delight greatly in the LORD; my soul rejoices in my God. For he has clothed me with garments of salvation and arrayed me in a robe of righteousness, as a bridegroom adorns his head like a priest, and as a bride adorns herself with her jewels" (Isaiah 61:10).

The robe of righteousness is also a New Testament picture for the justified. It is often tied to a comparison with marriage. Paul spoke of Jesus as the bridegroom and the church as the bride: "Christ loved the church and gave himself up for her to make her holy, cleansing her by the washing with water through the word, and to present her to himself as a radiant church, without stain or wrinkle or any other blemish, but holy and blameless" (Ephesians

5:25-27). Jesus alluded to this picture in his parable of the wedding banquet: "When the king came in to see the guests, he noticed a man there who was not wearing wedding clothes" (Matthew 22:11). Jesus said that man was to be thrown "outside, into the darkness, where there will be weeping and gnashing of teeth" (verse 13).

Most of the references to white clothing in Revelation are references to believers who are already in heaven. Yet the white clothes already belong to the saints on earth. Jesus told the church at Sardis: "Yet you have a few people in Sardis who have not soiled their clothes. They will walk with me, dressed in white, for they are worthy. He who overcomes will, like them, be dressed in white. I will never blot out his name from the book of life" (Revelation 3:4,5).

Priests

Priest is another Bible term for the believer who has been justified through faith. John offered a doxology to Jesus for making us priests in God's kingdom: "To him who loves us and has freed us from our sins by his blood, and has made us to be a kingdom and priests to serve his God and Father—to him be glory and power for ever and ever! Amen" (Revelation 1:5,6).

Unfortunately, misunderstanding about this word often prevents Christians from thinking of themselves as priests of God. Too often we think of priests in terms of those mentioned in the Old Testament. Those priests offered sacrifices on behalf of the people to prefigure what the coming Savior would do on behalf of the whole world. The Roman Catholic Church aggravates this misunderstanding by calling their clergymen *priests*. Rome teaches that people must play a part in their own salvation by making sacrifices to God. So their priests, in their view, are making sacrifices for themselves and on behalf of their people to gain a part of their forgiveness.

The Bible has a radically different view. After the coming of Christ, no more priests, in the style of the Old Testament priests, are needed. The Old Testament law that established the priesthood was "only a shadow of the good things that are coming—not the realities themselves" (Hebrews 10:1). The various Old Testament ceremonies and sacrifices were "a shadow of the things that were to come; the reality, however, is found in Christ" (Colossians 2:17). They served their purpose in pointing ahead to the sacrifice of Christ. But now that Christ has come, no more sacrifices for sin are needed.

The coming of the Great High Priest, Jesus Christ, did away with the Old Testament priesthood and all of its sacrifices for sins. This is the consistent message of Scripture:

> Day after day, every priest stands and performs his religious duties; again and again he offers the same sacrifices, which can never take away sins. But when this priest [Jesus] had offered for all time one sacrifice for sins, he sat down at the right hand of God. . . . By one sacrifice he has made perfect forever those who are being made holy. . . . And where these [sins and lawless acts] have been forgiven, there is no longer any sacrifice for sin. (Hebrews 10:11-18)

Yet there are priests in the New Testament. All of God's people are priests. Peter wrote, "You also, like living stones, are being built into a spiritual house to be a holy priesthood, offering spiritual sacrifices acceptable to God through Jesus Christ" (1 Peter 2:5). Luther was insistent that all believers consider themselves priests:

> A priest, especially in the New Testament, was not made but was born. He was created, not ordained. He was born not indeed of flesh, but through a birth of the Spirit, by water and Spirit in the washing of regeneration [John 3:6f.; Titus 3:5f.]. Indeed, all Christians are priests, and all priests are Christians. Worthy of anathema is any assertion that a priest is anything else than a Christian. For such an assertion has no support in the Word of God and is based only on human opinions.[24]

New Testament priests also offer sacrifices. But the sacrifices we make are not sacrifices to pay for sins; Jesus did that. "He has appeared once for all at the end of the ages to do away with sin by the sacrifice of himself" (Hebrews 9:26). Our only sacrifices as priests of God are thank offerings. We live to praise Jesus for his completed sacrifice. "But you are a chosen people, a royal priesthood, a holy nation, a people belonging to God, that you may declare the praises of him who called you out of darkness into his wonderful light" (1 Peter 2:9).

Our priestly thank offerings flow directly from the mercy of God shown to us in justification. Paul wrote, "Therefore, I urge you, brothers, in view of God's mercy, to offer your bodies as living sacrifices, holy and pleasing to God—this is your spiritual act of worship" (Romans 12:1). The Christian life is one of total and perpetual sacrifice. "Be imitators of God, therefore, as dearly loved children and live a life of love, just as Christ loved us and gave himself up for us as a fragrant offering and sacrifice to God" (Ephesians 5:1,2).

As members of the universal priesthood of believers, our sacrifices include our good works, our generous gifts, our service to our neighbors, and above all the glory we bring to God by proclaiming justification to the world. But there is another important part of our priestly service: prayer. When we pray for ourselves and others, we share the same privilege as Old Testament priests and our Great High Priest, Jesus Christ. Since we have been justified by faith, "we have gained access by faith into this grace in which we now stand" (Romans 5:2). We can do something no unbeliever can. We can come directly before the throne of God, and in the name of Jesus, we can have the confidence that our every prayer will be heard and answered. "In him and through faith in him we may approach God with freedom and confidence" (Ephesians 3:12).

This high privilege of every believer-priest flows directly from the completed sacrifice of our Great High Priest, Jesus.

> Therefore, since we have a great high priest who has gone through the heavens, Jesus the Son of God, let us hold firmly to the faith we profess. For we do not have a high priest who is unable to sympathize with our weaknesses, but we have one who has been tempted in every way, just as we are—yet was without sin. Let us then approach the throne of grace with confidence, so that we may receive mercy and find grace to help us in our time of need. (Hebrews 4:14-16)

Scripture invites us to make use of our priestly privilege of prayer. Paul wrote, "I urge, then, first of all, that request, prayers, intercession and thanksgiving be made for everyone—for kings and all those in authority, that we may live peaceful and quiet lives in all godliness and holiness" (1 Timothy 2:1,2). Peter tied our prayers to our sacrifice of godly living: "The end of all things is near. Therefore be clear minded and self-controlled so that you can pray" (1 Peter 4:7). James added, "Therefore confess your sins to each other and pray for each other so that you may be healed. The prayer of a righteous man is powerful and effective" (James 5:16).

In God's kingdom, the kingdom of those who have been justified through faith, all are priests. Every Christian offers sacrifices of thank offerings by living a life that glorifies God and by witnessing to his Great High Priest, Jesus Christ. And when obstacles get in the way of our priestly service, we have the priestly privilege of prayer, direct access to the right hand of God, where our High Priest is seated. The privilege and blessings of this priesthood are ours through faith.

Members of God's family

Earthly families offer stability, mutual encouragement, a sense of belonging, and a place to come back to when the world becomes too difficult. Family means comfortableness; wherever family is, that is home. All these blessings and more derive from our membership in the family of God. "How great is the love the Father has lavished on us, that we should be called children of God! And that is what we are!" (1 John 3:1).

Being a member of God's family is a status enjoyed only by those who have been justified through faith. Like saints and priests, the justified are fully and completely sons and daughters of God. God has no stepsons or stepdaughters. God's declaration of justification has taken us out of the control of Satan and placed us firmly into God's household. "Consequently, you are no longer foreigners and aliens, but fellow citizens with God's people and members of God's household" (Ephesians 2:19). "You are all sons of God through faith in Christ Jesus" (Galatians 3:26).

The ties we have to God's family through faith are stronger than the blood bonds we share in our human relationships. "To all who received him [Jesus], to those who believed in his name, he gave the right to become children of God—children born not of natural descent, nor of human decision or a husband's will, but born of God" (John 1:12,13). The righteousness that God has declared to be ours through faith is the bond that ties us to our heavenly Father. "Both the one who makes men holy and those who are made holy are of the same family. So Jesus is not ashamed to call them brothers" (Hebrews 2:11).

As the bond among God's family members is stronger, so the blessings of being brothers and sisters of Jesus Christ are even greater than those of earthly families (see Romans 9:8). Jesus made this comparison: "If you then, though you are evil, know how to give good gifts to your children, how much more will your Father in heaven give the Holy Spirit to those who ask him!" (Luke 11:13). David professed greater security in God's family than in his earthly relationships: "Though my father and mother forsake me, the LORD will receive me" (Psalm 27:10).

Heirs

Closely connected to the status of family membership with God is the inheritance God's children receive. Paul made this connection: "The Spirit himself testifies with our spirit that we are God's children. Now if we are children, then we are heirs—heirs of God and co-heirs with Christ" (Romans 8:16,17).

As with justification by faith, our status as heirs is not something we earn or gradually grow into. As soon as we are converted, we have the full rights of sons. "He saved us through the washing of rebirth and renewal by the Holy

Spirit, whom he poured out on us generously through Jesus Christ our Savior, so that, having been justified by his grace, we might become heirs having the hope of eternal life" (Titus 3:5-7). This was true of Old Testament believers like Noah: "By his faith he condemned the world and became heir of the righteousness that comes by faith" (Hebrews 11:7). The same inheritance comes to New Testament believers like you and me: "If you belong to Christ, then you are Abraham's seed, and heirs according to the promise" (Galatians 3:29).

Most obviously our inheritance consists of our final reward in heaven. "Listen, my dear brothers: Has not God chosen those who are poor in the eyes of the world to be rich in faith and to inherit the kingdom he promised those who love him?" (James 2:5). "Now if we are children, then we are heirs—heirs of God and co-heirs with Christ, if indeed we share in his sufferings in order that we may also share in his glory" (Romans 8:17). But already on this earth there are privileges that come to those who are heirs of God. God takes special care of his own. "Are not all angels ministering spirits sent to serve those who will inherit salvation?" (Hebrews 1:14). We live with the daily comfort that our loving Father manages and controls life's worst difficulties for our eventual good. "'The Lord disciplines those he loves, and he punishes everyone he accepts as a son.' Endure hardship as discipline; God is treating you as sons" (Hebrews 12:6,7).

Unity with God

Behind all the titles that Scripture confers on believers—saints, priests, children of God, and heirs—lies the truth that through justification they share a very close union with God. The essential element of that union with God is holiness, that is, the righteousness God now counts as ours in justification by faith.

The holiness we share with God, of course, is the basis for the unity we share with all our fellow believers. The distinction between Jews and Gentiles was erased by Jesus whose righteousness is credited equally to both through faith: "His purpose was to create in himself one new man out of the two, thus making peace, and in this one body to reconcile both of them to God through the cross" (Ephesians 2:15,16). In fact, the unity that the righteousness of Christ brings about eliminates every division of race, sex, and social class: "There is neither Jew nor Greek, slave nor free, male nor female, for you are all one in Christ Jesus" (Galatians 3:28).

Since our unity with our fellow Christians and with God himself is established through faith, every means by which the Holy Spirit creates and strengthens faith produces such unity. Paul said, for example, that union with God and fellow believers is offered and given to us in the Holy Supper: "Is not the cup of thanksgiving for which we give thanks a participation in the blood of Christ? And is not the bread that we break a participation in the body of Christ? Because there is one loaf, we, who are many, are one body, for we all partake of the one loaf" (1 Corinthians 10:16,17).

The gospel's call to faith and Baptism's power also confer unity with God and believers. "There is one body and one Spirit—just as you were called to one hope when you were called—one Lord, one faith, one baptism; one God and Father of all, who is over all and through all and in all" (Ephesians 4:4-6).

Paul expressed this unity in a concrete way by referring to all believers as the body of Christ and to Christ as the head of the body. "The body is a unit, though it is made up of many parts; and though all its parts are many, they form one body. So it is with Christ. For we were all baptized by one Spirit into one body—whether Jews or Greeks, slave or free—and we were all given the one Spirit to drink. Now you are the body of Christ, and each one of you is a part of it" (1 Corinthians 12:12,13,27). "So in Christ we who are many form one body, and each member belongs to all the others" (Romans 12:5).

Our new union with God through justification is so indescribably intimate that it has been called the *mystic union*. That term comes from Paul's comparison of the union between Christ and believers to the one-flesh union of marriage. He wrote, "For the husband is the head of the wife as Christ is the head of the church, his body, of which he is the Savior" (Ephesians 5:23). He went on to say that the closeness of this union is a mystery:

> After all, no one ever hated his own body, but he feeds and cares for it, just as Christ does the church—for we are members of his body. "For this reason a man will leave his father and mother and be united to his wife, and the two will become one flesh." This is a profound mystery—but I am talking about Christ and the church. (Ephesians 5:29-32)

Jesus spoke about this mystic union in the upper room. He said the unity among believers is the same as the union between himself and the Father. Jesus prayed to the Father: "My prayer is not for them alone. I pray also for those who will believe in me through their message, that all of them may be one, Father, just as you are in me and I am in you. May they also be in us so that the world may believe that you have sent me" (John 17:20,21).

Full, free, and immediate justification by faith is rich with assurances from God. In God's declaration of "not guilty" for the sinner, he also commits to us the status of saint, priest, family member, and heir. About the time we think we have begun to grasp all this, Jesus mystifies us by telling us we share the same union with him that he shares with God the Father. It is amazing grace, to be sure. But a wise and loving God knows we need every one of these assurances in the face of Satan's constant accusation. We need every promise, every conferred title, every declared status to be sure that God has taken us to be his own in Christ and will not let go.

What is the final status of the justified?

We will have the white-robed perfection of heaven.

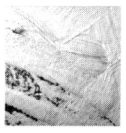

10

What Is the Final Status of the Justified?

The image of Christ

In heaven God will make us to be what he on earth declared us to be. The people God declared holy in the blood of Christ, he will make holy in the image of Christ. Body and soul we will possess the image of Jesus, who became human body and soul to redeem us. "Dear friends, now we are children of God, and what we will be has not yet been made known. But we know that when he appears, we shall be like him, for we shall see him as he is" (1 John 3:2).

At heaven's door God will make the gradual process of sanctification complete in us. God will make each of us to be what he declared us to be through faith in Christ Jesus. At Jesus' resurrection, God rendered his justifying verdict, "Not guilty!" At our resurrection, God will make us to be personally holy. "For you died, and your life is now hidden with Christ in God. When Christ, who is your life, appears, then you also will appear with him in glory" (Colossians 3:3,4).

To have Christ's image fully restored in us means that we will no longer have our sinful nature or the constant warfare it wages against the new self. The image of God consists of perfect knowledge and personal holiness. Already now the new self "is being renewed in knowledge in the image of its Creator" (Colossians 3:10). But in heaven our knowledge will be perfectly renewed as it was in the Garden before the fall into sin. "Now we see but a poor reflection as in a mirror; then we shall see face to face. Now I know in part; then I shall know fully, even as I am fully known" (1 Corinthians 13:12).

At the moment we were justified through faith, the Holy Spirit created a new self in us. That new self was "created to be like God in true righteousness and holiness" (Ephesians 4:24). Even though the new self is a perfect creation of God already now, the persistence of the old Adam in us keeps us from living truly holy lives. But in heaven we will become truly righteous. The righteousness declared in justification will become inherent. David lived with this confidence in the final resurrection: "And I—in righteousness I will see your face; when I awake, I will be satisfied with seeing your likeness" (Psalm 17:15).

White robes

The Bible pictures the righteous image of Christ, which we will fully possess in heaven, as white clothing. The white robes that justification draped us in already on earth will become our permanent possession in heaven. "Yet you have a few people in Sardis who have not soiled their clothes. They will walk with me, dressed in white, for they are worthy. He who overcomes will, like them, be dressed in white. I will never blot out his name from the book of life" (Revelation 3:4,5). In John's vision of heaven, he saw the blessed wearing white robes: "Then one of the elders asked me, 'These in white robes—who are they, and where did they come from?' I answered, 'Sir, you know.' And he said, 'These are they who have come out of the great tribulation; they have washed their robes and made them white in the blood of the Lamb'" (Revelation 7:13,14).

The perfection of believers in heaven is also pictured as bright, even blinding, light. This is consistent with the Bible's many glimpses of God's holiness on earth. Moses' face reflected the glory of God's perfection when he came down from the mount (Exodus 34:29-35; 2 Corinthians 3:13). Jesus appeared with Moses and Elijah on the Mount of Transfiguration in similar splendor (Luke 9:29-31). Daniel says the saints in heaven will likewise reflect the glory of God's holiness: "Those who are wise will shine like the brightness of the heavens, and those who lead many to righteousness, like the stars for ever and ever" (Daniel 12:3).

Bride of the Lamb

In chapter 9 we noted how justification unites believers in the church with Christ in a holy marriage. In heaven this marriage will be consummated. In Revelation the pictures of white clothing and the marriage to the Lamb are connected: "'Let us rejoice and be glad and give him glory! For the wedding of the Lamb has come, and his bride has made herself ready. Fine linen, bright and clean, was given her to wear.' (Fine linen stand for the righteous acts of the saints)" (Revelation 19:7,8).

Later John witnessed the eternal honeymoon of the bride of Christ: "'Come, I will show you the bride, the wife of the Lamb.' And he carried me away in the Spirit to a mountain great and high, and showed me the Holy City, Jerusalem, coming down out of heaven from God" (Revelation 21:9,10).

Spiritual bodies

When God obliterates sin in us, the consequences of sin will also be gone. The ravages of sin and its consequences on our bodies will disappear. "So it will be with the resurrection of the dead. The body that is sown is perishable, it is raised imperishable; it is sown in dishonor, it is raised in glory; it is sown in weakness, it is raised in power; it is sown a natural body, it is raised a spiritual body" (1 Corinthians 15:42-44). In others words, our bodies will be like Christ's resurrected body. "Our citizenship is in heaven. And we eagerly await a Savior from there, the Lord Jesus Christ, who, by the power that enables him to bring everything under his control, will transform our lowly bodies so that they will be like his glorious body" (Philippians 3:20,21).

Our new spiritual bodies will derive their life from God and be devoted in service to God. The saints in heaven are "before the throne of God and serve him day and night in his temple. . . . The Lamb at the center of the throne will be their shepherd; he will lead them to springs of living water" (Revelation 7:15,17). We will not need marriage in heaven. "When the dead rise, they will neither marry nor be given in marriage; they will be like the angels in heaven" (Mark 12:25).

The external troubles that result from sin will also be gone. "[God] will wipe every tear from their eyes. There will be no more death or mourning or crying or pain, for the old order of things has passed away" (Revelation 21:4). "No longer will there be any curse" (Revelation 22:3). Paul looked forward to an eternity devoid of the troubles of this life: "We ourselves, who have the firstfruits of the Spirit, groan inwardly as we wait eagerly for our adoption as sons, the redemption of our bodies" (Romans 8:23).

Judges

Since we will share in Jesus' holiness, we will also share in his work for an eternity. A part of Christ's work is to serve as judge. Our Lord promised us: "I confer on you a kingdom, just as my Father conferred one on me, so that you may eat and drink at my table in my kingdom and sit on thrones, judging the twelve tribes of Israel" (Luke 22:29,30). Paul rhetorically challenged the Corinthians, "Do you not know that the saints will judge the world?" (1 Corinthians 6:2). In his vision John saw saints in heaven judging: "I saw thrones on which were seated those who had been given authority to judge. . . . They came to life and reigned with Christ a thousand years" (Revelation 20:4).

Priests

Those who caricature the saints in heaven as serenely bored have not read the Holy Scriptures. Cartoons that pose the blessed with halos on their heads, floating on clouds, and playing harps have no scriptural warrant. We who possess the image of our holy God will be constantly and joyfully occupied. Not only will we be judges seated with Christ, we will be active priests. "Blessed and holy are those who have part in the first resurrection. The second death has no power over them, but they will be priests of God and of Christ and will reign with him for a thousand years" (Revelation 20:6).

Our time in heaven will be spent in meaningful service and praise of the God who justified us in Christ. The blissful presence of God will elicit our never-ending service. "The throne of God and of the Lamb will be in the city, and his servants will serve him. They will see his face, and his name will be on their foreheads. There will be no more night. They will not need the light of a lamp or the light of the sun, for the Lord God will give them light. And they will reign for ever and ever" (Revelation 22:3-5).

Justification is an anchor

God keeps his promises. Justification by faith anchors us to his fulfilled promises of the past. And justification by faith anchors us to the reliability of his promises of future glory. All the promises of future life are tied directly to God's declaration of righteousness to us right now. Certainly Luther and the reformers were right when they observed from Scripture that justification by faith is the central teaching of Christianity. God give us grace always to regard it as such.

> Jesus, your blood and righteousness
> My beauty are, my glorious dress;
> Mid flaming worlds, in these arrayed,
> With joy shall I lift up my head.
>
> Bold shall I stand in that great day—
> Who can a word against me say?

Fully through you absolved I am
From sin and fear, from guilt and shame.

When from the dust of death I rise
To claim my mansion in the skies,
E'en then this shall be all my plea:
Jesus has lived and died for me. (CW 376:1,2,5)

Endnotes

[1] Martin Luther, *Luther's Works*, edited by Jaroslav Pelikan and Helmut T. Lehmann, American Edition, Vol. 26 (St. Louis: Concordia Publishing House; Philadelphia: Fortress Press, 1955–1986), p. 9.

[2] Formula of Concord, Epitome, Article III:7, *The Book of Concord: The Confessions of the Evangelical Lutheran Church*, translated and edited by Theodore G. Tappert (Philadelphia: Fortress Press, 1959), p. 473.

[3] *What Luther Says: An Anthology*, compiled by Ewald M. Plass, Vol. 2 (St. Louis: Concordia Publishing House, 1959), p. 701.

[4] *Luther's Works*, Vol. 27, p. 242.

[5] *Luther's Works*, Vol. 26, pp. 183,184.

[6] *Luther's Works*, Vol. 27, p. 242.

[7] Joh. P. Meyer, *Ministers of Christ: A Commentary on the Second Epistle of Paul to the Corinthians*, (Milwaukee: Northwestern Publishing House, 1963), p. 112.

[8] *What Luther Says*, p. 703.

[9] *What Luther Says*, p. 704.

[10] Formula of Concord, Solid Declaration, Article III:6, Tappert, p. 540.
[11] Armin W. Schuetze, "The Presupposition of Justification: The Sin of Man and the Holiness of God," in *His Pardoning Grace*, edited by Siegbert W. Becker (Milwaukee: Northwestern Publishing House, 1966), p. 3.
[12] *Christian Worship: A Lutheran Hymnal* (Milwaukee: Northwestern Publishing House, 1993), p. 15.
[13] Armin Schuetze, *His Pardoning Grace*, p. 3.
[14] *Luther's Works*, Vol. 26, p. 126.
[15] Formula of Concord, Solid Declaration, Article III:15, Tappert, p. 541.
[16] *What Luther Says*, p. 709.
[17] Formula of Concord, Solid Declaration, Article XI:15, Tappert, p. 619.
[18] Formula of Concord, Solid Declaration, Article XI:28, Tappert, p. 620.
[19] Apology of the Augsburg Confession, Article IV:103, Tappert, pp. 121,122.
[20] Large Catechism, Part III:88, Tappert, p. 432.
[21] *What Luther Says*, p. 707.
[22] Augsburg Confession, Article IV:1, Tappert, p. 30.
[23] *Luther's Works*, Vol. 24, pp. 170,171.
[24] *Luther's Works*, Vol. 40, p. 19.

For Further Reading

Augsburg Confession, Article IV; Apology to the Augsburg Confession, Article IV; Formula of Concord, Solid Declaration, Article III. *The Book of Concord: The Confessions of the Evangelical Lutheran Church.* Translated and edited by Theodore G. Tappert. Philadelphia: Fortress Press, 1959.

Becker, Siegbert. "Universal Justification." in *Our Great Heritage.* Vol. 3. Edited by Lyle W. Lange. Milwaukee: Northwestern Publishing House, 1991.

Dobberstein, Leroy A. "The Doctrine of Justification in the Light of Present Problems." *Wisconsin Lutheran Quarterly*, Vol. 84, No. 1 (Winter 1987).

Pieper, Francis. *Christian Dogmatics.* Vol. 2. St. Louis: Concordia Publishing House, 1951.

Scripture Index

Genesis
 3—23
 3:1—24
 3:6—24
 3:12—27
 15—13
 15:6—13,17

Exodus
 34:29-35—119

Leviticus
 11:44—37

Psalms
 11:7—36
 13:5—58
 17:15—118
 27:10—110
 32—13
 49:7-9—38
 51:7—41
 85:8—104
 145:17—35

Proverbs
 14:12—24

Isaiah
 6:3—35
 9:6—39
 28:16—59
 53:7,8—40
 61:10—104

Jeremiah
 31:34—18

Ezekiel
 18:32—50

Daniel
  12:3—119

Habakkuk
  2:4—16

Matthew
  1:23—39
  3:15—43
  5:17—42
  5:44,45—94
  5:48—30
  6:24—70
  8:10—70
  9:2—73
  12:20—73
  12:33-37—94
  15:28—70
  22:11—105
  22:13—105
  25:31-46—94,95
  27:46—40
  27:52—102

Mark
  9:24—71
  12:25—121
  16:16—70

Luke
  2:27—43
  2:41-52—43
  9:29-31—119
  11:13—110
  16:15—93
  18:11,12—29
  18:14—17

  22:29,30—121
  22:42—40
  23:43—71
  24:47—51

John
  1:1—39
  1:12,13—110
  1:14—39
  1:16-18—38
  1:29—41,50,51
  3:6,7—107
  3:16—36,49
  3:18—45,69
  8:46—43
  13:35—94
  14:1—58
  14:9—39
  15:16—62
  17:20,21—113

Acts
  3:15—41
  4:12—45
  6:3—89
  13:37-39—14
  20:27—97
  20:28—41

Romans
  1—31
  1:7—102
  1:16,17—67
  1:17—16
  2—31
  3-5—31,81
  3:10-12—89

3:20—31
3:21—16
3:21,22—16
3:22,23—89
3:22-24—55
3:26—37
3:28—53,60
4—17
4:3—13,17,44
4:5—17,58,60
4:6—13
4:22-24—18
4:23,24—44
4:23-25—14
4:25—40
5:1—17,73
5:1,2—9
5:2—73,108
5:6—40
5:8—37
5:9—41
5:9,10—19
5:12-19—53-55
5:15—54,55
5:18—52
5:19—39,54
5:20—51
6:1—81
6:6,7—81
6:22—82
7:18—85
7:18,19—85
7:21-24—85
7:24,25—85
8:7—61
8:7,8—25
8:16,17—110

8:17—111
8:23—121
8:27—104
9:8—110
12:1—84,107
12:2—81
12:5—113
15:5—55
15:16—78

1 Corinthians
1:2—102
2:9,10—62
3:1-3—88
6:2—104,121
6:11—78
10:16,17—112
12—72
12:3—62
12:12,13—113
12:27—113
13:12—118
15:17—14
15:42-44—120

2 Corinthians
1:1—102
3:13—119
5:15—50,51
5:18—18
5:18,19—19,52
5:19—51
5:21—40,44
13:13—103

Galatians
2:15,16—12,59
2:16—60

2:21—17
3:10—38
3:10,11—30
3:13—38,40
3:26—109
3:28—112
3:29—111
4:4,5—43
5:1—73
5:4—16

Ephesians
1:1—102
1:4,5—36
1:9—37
1:13—62
1:18,19—104
2:3—27
2:8,9—61
2:9,10—83
2:15,16—112
2:19—109
3:12—108
3:17,18—104
4:4-6—112
4:12,13—80
4:13,14—88
4:22-24—80
4:24—118
5:1,2—84,107
5:19,20—84
5:23—113
5:25,26—78
5:25-27—104
5:26—41
5:29-32—113
6:10-13—86

Philippians
1:1—102
1:9-11—86
2:8—40
2:12,13—83
3:7-9—46
3:8,9—15,79
3:12—79
3:12-14—87
3:20,21—120

Colossians
1:2—102
1:19,20—51
1:21,22—19
2:14—51
2:17—106
3:3—93
3:3,4—118
3:9,10—80
3:10—118
3:17—84

1 Thessalonians
4:1,3,7—90
5:16-18—84

1 Timothy
2:1,2—108
2:4—49
2:5—39
3:9—88
4:15,16—88
5:10—103

2 Timothy
1:6—72

2:13—35
2:19—93
2:21—77
3:16—97

Titus
2:11,12—80
2:14—41
3:5—59
3:5,6—107
3:5-7—111

Hebrews
1:14—111
2:11—110
2:14,15—40
4:13—26
4:14-16—108
4:15—43
5:12-14—88
6:1—87
6:11,12—87
9:26—50,107
9:28—41
10:1—106
10:5-7—39
10:9,10—41
10:11-18—106
10:14—79
11:6—97
11:7—111
12:6,7—111

James
1:22—96
2:5—111
2:10—30
2:14-17—95

2:18—96
2:24—95
2:26—96
5:16—109

1 Peter
1:19—43
1:20—37
2:5—106
2:9—107
4:7—108

2 Peter
1:10—95
3:9—49

1 John
1:7—41
1:8,9—26,89
2:2—50
2:3—95
3:1—109
3:2—117
3:14—95
4:16—35,59

Jude
14—102

Revelation
1:5,6—105
3:4,5—105,119
3:16—70
4:8—35
7:13,14—119
7:15,17—120
19:7,8—120

20:4—121
20:6—122
21:4—121

21:9,10—120
22:3—121
22:3-5—122

Subject Index

abortion, condoned by churches 26,28
alien righteousness 15-17,42
America, post-Christian 8,20, 64,65
Apology to the Augsburg Confession 51
Apostles' Creed 55
Arminianism 8
atonement, limited 50
Augsburg Confession 67
Augsburg Confession, Apology to the 51

Baptist churches 64,65
blaming others 27,28,31
bodies, spiritual 120,121

Catholic Church. See Roman Catholic Church
Christianity, levels of 71,72
churches promoting sins 26,27
cliques within congregations 28
comparing 28-31
confession 27,108,109
confirmation syndrome 87

decision theology 27,64,65
denial 25-27,31
divorce, unscriptural, condoned by churches 26

Eastern mysticism 8,45
Evangelical churches 64,65

faith
    fruits of 94-98
    journey to 69,70
    personal 8,9
    power of 59
    saving, created in us by God 61,62
faith and justification 58-67

faith and unity 112,113
fall into sin 15,23-32,80
favoritism among Christians 30
Fifth Petition of the Lord's Prayer 52
finger pointing 27,28
First Commandment 24
forgiveness,
   full 70,71
   word pictures for 7,101-114
Formula of Concord 50,51
fornication, condoned by churches 26
Fundamentalism 8

God, pictured as kindly grandfather 37
God's family, members 109-111
good works 59,78,83,93-98
gospel for all people of all time 13,49-52
gradualism 71-74

heirs 110,111
Holiness denominations 89,90
holiness 111-114
   personal 118
Holy Communion 66
holy ones 101-104
Holy Spirit, work of 77-90
homosexuality, condoned by churches 26,28
humanism 8

image of God 80,117,118
indulgences 71
inheritance 110,111
installation of Lutheran pastors and teachers 51
Islam 45

Jesus
   as bringer of salvation 38-47
   as Great High Priest 106-109
   as substitute 39-45
   as true God and true man 38-44
Joint Declaration on the Doctrine of Justification (JDDJ) 62-64
judges 121
judgment, human 25
justification
   forensic nature of 12
   gradual 71-74
   instant 69-74
   invisible 93,97,98
   visible 94-98
   worldly 23-32
justification and Easter 14,16,52,57,58
justification and the gospel 13
justification as anchor 122,123
justification as cornerstone of the church's teaching 7,19,20,122,123
justification as synonym for *sanctification* 78

justification brings change 18,19
justification defined 11-13,17
justification distinguished from *sanctification* 78-80,82
justification in Scripture 17,18

Large Catechism 52
law, ignorance of 29,30
levels of Christianity 71,72
liberalism 8
limited atonement 50
love, God's universal, 49-51
Lutheran church 11,13,27,62-64
Lutheran Confessions 13,50,58
Lutheran World Federation (LWF) 62-64

many, Paul's use of the word 53-55
marriage of Christ and believers 104,105,119,120
masses, Roman Catholic 71
members of God's family 109-111
Meyer, John 18,19
Middle Ages 7,8
modernism 8
Moody Bible Institute 30
Moody, Dr. Dwight 30
motivation for moral living 73,74
motivation, God's, to justify us 35-47

mystic union 113,114
mysticism, Eastern 8,45

Native American traditions 45
nature of God 35,36
new self 80-90,118

obedience
  Jesus' active 39,42-45
  Jesus' passive 39-43
objective justification 52-55, 57,58,66
ordination of Lutheran pastors 51
original sin denied by churches 27
orthodoxy, dead 8

penances, Roman Catholic 71
perfectionism 89,90
Pietism 8
piety, false 37
plan of salvation 36,37
pluralism 45,65
post-Christian America 8,20, 64,65
prayer 108,109
predestination, double 50
priests 105-109,121,122
psychology, human 23-32

rationalism 8
rationalizing 24,25,28,31
reconciliation 19
Reformation, Lutheran 8,53,81,122

Reformed church 50,64,65
righteousness
    alien 15-17,42
    credited by faith 17,18,44
    inherent 15
    robe of 104,105,118,119
"Rock of Ages, Cleft for Me" 29,82
Roman Catholic Church 44, 53,62-64,71,102,103,105, 106

Sacrament of Holy Baptism 66
sacrifices offered by priests 105-109
saint worship, Roman Catholic 71
saints 101-104,120,121
sanctification 77-90
sanctification as synonym for *justification* 78
sanctification distinguished from *justification* 78-80,82
Satan and attacks on justification 8,9,12,37
Schuetze, Armin 26
sectarianism 8

self-justification 23-32
sinner-saint 84-90
sins, promoted in churches 26-28
situational ethics 25,28
Small Catechism 62
Speratus, Paul 46,47
Spirit-baptized Christians 72
state of grace 73
status, sinner's, changed before God 12,13,18,19
subjective justification 58-62

Third Article of the Apostles' Creed 62
traditions, Native American 45

unity with God 111-114
universal priesthood of believers 105-109

visible church 20

water-baptized Christians 72
white robes 104,105,118,119
work-righteousness 53